THE VISUAL GUIDE TO

UNDERSTANDING

PROPHECY & THE BOOK OF REVELATION

THE TIMES

- To God Be The Glory -

*Dedicated to the
Tribulation saints.*

*Seek God first,
and highest, above all.*

ISBN: 978-0-9844683-8-6 (Hardcover BW)

* **There is a *LOT* of misinformation and preconceived ideas out about some of these perspectives and points, but please consider what the Bible says about all of these.**

This material is presented as serious food for serious thought, and as Berean research submitted for review and further research. No determinations are made; it is not a prediction.

- Much time, care, effort, and prayer has gone into the research for this timeline and compilation, comparing a variety of prophetic viewpoints from a Scriptural foundation.

- If there are any demonstratable corrections or well-cited adjustments needed, we will readily update accordingly.

- I ask that you also be as the Bereans, who *"...received the word with all readiness of mind, and searched the scriptures daily, whether those things were so."* - Acts 17:11

Table of Contents

PAST HISTORY

Introduction 1
Fallen Angels 7
Sodom & Gomorrah 8
Sumer & Babel 9
Babel's Symbols.................... 12

Solomon's Apostasy............14
Babylonian Captivity 15
Time of Christ........................16
The Early Church..................17
The False Church..................18

CURRENT HISTORY

Satan's Chess Game 22
Technology Role 28
Watching 32

The Last Generation 36
Signs Fulfilled 42
Days of Noah & Lot 49

FUTURE HISTORY

Middle East Wars...................51
Blood Moons..........................55
Islam's Role............................56
Rewards 57
Tribulation Time & Dates....59
The Book of Revelation 60
1,2,3 - Seven Churches 61
4 - The Church In Heaven...64
5 - The Lamb.........................70
6 - The Seal Judgments 72
7 - The 144,000 78
8 - Trumpets 1-4 80
9 - Trumpets 5-6 83
10 - The Seven Thunders....86
11 - The 7th Trumpet..........87
    Two Witnesses 88
    The Antichrist.................89
    Trib. Deceptions 93

12 - Tribulation Midpoint...97
    Woman & Dragon.........99
13 - The Beasts 101
    Mark of the Beast....... 102
    Image of the Beast.... 104
14 - Interlude...................... 105
15 - Just and True............... 108
16 - The Seven Bowls........ 109
17 - Harlot Destroyed....... 114
18 - Babylon Destroyed... 115
19 - Christ's Return 116
20 - Millennial Kingdom.. 120
    Judgment Day 124
21 - New Heaven & Earth. 127

INDEX........................... 139

Introduction

**" "*...which were men that had
understanding of the times,
to know what Israel ought to do...* " "**
- I Chron. 12:32

"the mystery of iniquity" vs. *"the mystery of Christ"*

If you want to have the best understanding of prophecy and the
end times, you have to step back and look at the whole picture
that Scripture paints of the overall times.

Understanding the End of the World is linked to understanding
what has been happening since the Beginning of the World;
only then will you have a proper perspective of why things
are happening the way they are, and where they are going.

History is not just a collection of random events that stumble
through time sequentially. No, history is the account of
"the mystery of iniquity" versus *"the mystery of Christ"*
- the record of Satan's working in the world (II Thess. 2:7)
versus God's working in the world and eternity (Eph. 3:9).

To that end, this book includes a variety of historical and
current back reference that is necessary toward having a better
understanding of what lies ahead. This knowledge and
understanding should then prudently affect how we live
our life in light of eternity, and the decisions and actions
we take in this present world.

1

Jesus warned His disciples that Satan's plan and working was much larger than they knew about. Satan has been scheming and working an occult (hidden) plan from the time of Creation to overthrow God and His promised Redeemer, Jesus Christ.

"For the mystery of iniquity doth already work: only he who now letteth will let, until he be taken out of the way. And then shall that Wicked be revealed, whom the Lord shall consume with the spirit of his mouth, and shall destroy with the brightness of his coming: Even him, whose coming is after the working of Satan with all power and signs and lying wonders." II Thess. 2:7-9

As we will examine in this book, Satan's workings extend beyond what most people attend to, or are aware of. We will also see that God gives Satan a wide degree of liberty, latitude, and power in this world - until a certain time when Christ sets up His kingdom.

The Bible also forewarns that Satan's hidden influence extends to very high and powerful positions. While there is little or nothing we can do about changing it, we can put on the armour of God to guard ourselves against the wiles and devices of Satan's plans. Of course, the first piece of armour listed is being girded with truth.

"Put on the whole armour of God, that ye may be able to stand against the wiles of the devil. For we wrestle not against flesh and blood, but against principalities, against powers, against the rulers of the darkness of this world, against spiritual wickedness in high places."
- Ephesians 6:11-12

If you do not understand the times from a Christian perspective, you will not know, notice, or defend against Satan's influences into your life and home. You will also not be very effective in knowing the directives that you should be allowing and following in your life.

🔑 Satan has a literal government / power structure, with a literal seat of power.
In Revelation, Christ mentioned that during the early church period, Satan's seat was located at Pergamos (*"...where Satan's seat is..."* - Rev. 2:13). He was refering to the Pergamon Altar to Zeus. This monumental altar depicted a sculpted frieze of the pantheon of gods. It has been excavated and restored at the Pergamon Museum, in Berlin, Germany, along with a reconstructed Ishtar Gate from Babylon.

🔑 The time of the Tribulation will not be secular. It will be overtly religious (occultic); a false 'messiah' revival, mainly coming to bear 3.5 years after the peace treaty with Israel, led by Antichrist (false messiah).

Satan counterfeits all details of the true, and will have false 'signs' that deceive the world to believe he is a messiah. This will be Satan's masterpiece orchestration; the world has not seen anything even close since just prior to Noah's Flood. It will challenge your perception of everything - and that is its goal.

Antichrist's deception will largely be in the realm of the occult / supernatural - so convincing, even Jesus said they would deceive true believers - *"if it were possible"* (e.g. if they hadn't been gathered to Him prior to Antichrist's revealing)** Matthew 24:24.

The Left Behind books give a false portrayal - do not read or rely on them for anything prophetic.

The Mark of the Beast is inherently a badge of allegiance, not a microchip - although that technology may be used for control measures.

*"Beloved, believe not every spirit, but try the spirits whether they are of God: because many false prophets are gone out into the world. Hereby know ye the Spirit of God: Every spirit that confesseth that Jesus Christ is come in the flesh is of God: And **every spirit that confesseth not that Jesus Christ is come in the flesh is not of God: and this is that spirit of antichrist,** whereof ye have heard that it should come; and even now **already is it in the world.** Ye are of God, little children, and have overcome them: because **greater is he that is in you, than he that is in the world."***

- I John 4:1-4

Fallen Angels

The Bible tells us that, for generations before Noah's Flood, fallen angels procreated with humans and produced distinct hybrid offspring.

"There were giants in the earth in those days; and also after that, when the sons of God came in unto the daughters of men, and they bare children to them, the same became mighty men which were of old, men of renown." - Genesis 6:5

The Bible tells us that Noah was a righteous man - and that his genetic lineage was not corrupted like others of his time.

"...Noah was a just man and perfect in his generations..." - Genesis 6:9

This was important to preserve a pure, undefiled bloodline from Adam that the future Messiah would come from. Satan's goal at the beginning was to not just corrupt mankind spiritually, but also literally - and he came really close...

"And God looked upon the earth, and, behold, it was corrupt; for all flesh had corrupted his way upon the earth." - Genesis 6:12

Only Noah was uncorrupted - spiritually and physically; God sent the Flood to destroy the corruption.

David & Giants

When the children of Israel came to Caanan, they encountered giants, known as the sons of Anak (Num 13:22,28,33). The predecessors of the Anakims were the Emims (Deut. 2:11), and were also giants. Another group of giants were called the Zamzummims (Deut. 2:20). King Og of Bashan was also one of those giants; his bed was 9 cubits long (13.5') (Deut. 3:11). Bashan was known as the land of the giants (Deut. 3:13). Goliath had several in his family (II Sam. 21). These all seem to be of the same result as prior to the Flood.

🔥 Sodom & Gomorrah

At Sodom, fallen angels were once again involved in fornication with humans *"going after strange flesh"* (Jude 1:7). This is why the men of Sodom lusted after the good angels when they came to get Lot's family. It was a demonic lust that had already been cultured in Sodom; it was also their cause for judgment.

These angels, which *"left their own habitation"*, (before and after the Flood) are already chained in darkness awaiting the final judgment day (Jude 1:6). This was the second time that fallen angels physically tried to corrupt mankind - spiritually, morally, and physically.

Christ came to earth, within visual range of Sodom, and sent His angels to gather His servant Lot and family out (Gen. 18) **before** He judged Sodom for their wickedness.

"If ye then be risen with Christ, seek those things which are above, where Christ sitteth on the right hand of God. Set your affection on things above, not on things on the earth." - Col 3:1-2

"Remember Lot's wife."
- Luke 17:32

Remember that the one who longed and lived for the world, from which she was to be rescued from, ended up not truly leaving. Even though she was not appointed to wrath, she ended up being left behind and appointed to the same end as those of the sinners.

Sumer & Babel

Sumer, the First Civilization

This was the first known civilization (3500BC – 1900BC) most known for the ziggurat of Ur - the capital city of the Sumerian civilization (Shinar, Gen. 11:2). Ur was originally Abraham's home town (Neh. 9:7), before God called him out of there to another land. The Sumerians extensively recorded, in their cuneiform libraries, the presence of the Anunnaki, which corrolate with the Biblical concept of fallen angels and their offspring. Historians readily agree that these Anunnaki were worshipped by the Sumerians as gods. This was around the same time period as the tower of Babel. Even after the Flood, the fallen angels continued to visit mankind.

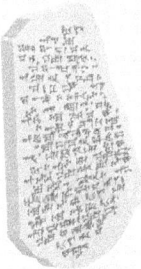

Advanced Information

Although there was no predecessor civilization, and they were apparently in their initial development, the Sumarians had precise information about the planets, equinoxes, and complex medical procedures. In their tablets they record that all of their knowledge came from the Anunnaki.

The Anunnaki also appear in the Babylonian creation myth, Enuma Elish.

The Annunaki are mentioned in The Epic of Gilgamesh when Utnapishtim tells the story of the flood.

Babylonian Nusku / Assyrian Nisroch

Laban's idols (Gen 11:29, 31:34) were most likely derived from the Anunnaki, and their kind.

Nimrod built the city of Babel (Gen 10-11). The purpose of the tower of Babel was to *"reach unto heaven"*, and to also prevent them from being scattered (11:4). It was man wanting to be their own god, and to govern without God.

Many ziggurats and pyramids are constructed to be spiritual staircases, approaching and merging the heavens and the earth.

Babel's gods

There were two main forces - a male and female force. Nimrod was regarded as the Sun-god, and his wife, Semiramis, was regarded as the Queen of Heaven, and later as Ishtar (Venus). The Egyptian main gods were these same two, just renamed: Osiris and Isis. Later, the Canaanite versions were Baal and Astarte.

The sun is a symbol of Satan, and is widely used in many secret societies as such; although most new initiates are not made aware (purposefully) of this satanic worship symbolism until higher degrees/levels.

Gods and Goddesses

Asherah, Astarte, Ashtoreth, Ishtar, Isis were all equivalent goddesses starting from this time. The root role was the 'Queen of the Stars/Heaven'.

Marduk / Merodach,
Lunar Babylonian god.

Ashur, the moon god of Ur, Sumerian Ninnar (Sin), Saturn, and Bel Enlil.

Sacred Bull

Early on, the bull was associated with lunar in Mesopotamia (its horns representing the crescent moon). In Egypt, the bull was worshiped as Apis.

The Hebrews were influenced by the Egyptian bull worship, and later made a similar molten calf (Exodus 32:4, Neh. 9:18).

Later, King Jeroboam made two calves of gold for Israel (I Kings 12:28) to worship. God referred to them as *"sin"* (vs. 30).

Molech / Chemosh

The worship of Caananite gods, including Moloch, involved sacrificing children by fire (2 Chr. 28:3, 33:6; Jer. 7:31, 19:2–6), usually the person's own children. The Canaanite (and later Carthaginian) deity Moloch was often depicted as a bull.

"And thou shalt not let any of thy seed pass through the fire to Moloch..." - Leviticus 18:21, Leviticus 20:2–5.

In the Old Testament, Gehenna was a valley by Jerusalem, where rituals of various false gods, including Moloch, took place.

These twisted and depraved rituals were often led and introduced by those in royalty (Solomon, I Kings 11:7; 33; etc.).

Planets appear as, and are also called, stars. Saturn, the 6th planet, represents Molech/Chiun.

God accused the Israelites of worshipping Remphan (Saturn/Molech) and his star: *"But ye have borne the tabernacle of your Moloch and Chiun your images, the star of your god, which ye made to yourselves."* -Amos 5:26. The New Testament martyr, Stephen, also proclaimed the same accusation, Acts 7:43 - *"...ye took up the tabernacle of Moloch, and the star of your god Remphan, figures which ye made to worship them..."*

Just prior to the Babylonian captivity, there were many in Israel who worshipped the queen of heaven, Ishtar (Jer. 44:17), and God even showed Ezekiel the elders and leaders who were involved in secret occult societies, worshipping pagan gods (Ezek. 8:8,22:6) in private and secretive gatherings.

Babel's Symbols

Not the Star of David

The star of Molech (and others idols) represents two triangles - the expression of 'as above, so below' - a unifying and synthesis of the heavenly and the earthly forces; merging the upward and downward forces. One triangle points up, the other down. It also represents the union of the male and female forces, usually Baal/Molech & Ishtar/Ashtoreth.

The ying and yang from Taoism would be the equivalent symbol/concept.

The Masonic checkerboard tile floors are another example.

God even accused the Israelites of worshipping Remphan (Saturn/Molech) and his star (Amos 5:26). The martyr, Stephen, also proclaimed the same accusation, Acts 7:43 - *"...ye took up the tabernacle of Moloch, and the star of your god Remphan, **figures which ye made to worship them**..."*

The hexagram (6) represents 666: 6 triangles outside, pointing outward. 6 lines make up the whole symbol. 6 intersections.

The star of Molech is often referred by those in Freemasonry as the Seal of Solomon, David's Shield, or the Talisman of Saturn.

Occult symbols are how the more-trained occult adherants recognize the activity of other groups, even if they don't know a connection between their groups. The use of the occult symbols is all they need to identify friend or foe to their esoteric goals. Broadcasting of the symbols in large venues is not for the public - it is for identification of who has condoned the venue and efforts.

*"...I would have you wise unto that which is good, and **simple concerning evil**. And the God of peace shall bruise Satan under your feet shortly. The grace of our Lord Jesus Christ be with you. Amen."* - Roman 16:19-20

If you need additional research on some of these subjects, always use Christian discernment sources.

Hat Tip

When one examines the multiple occult symbols used on American money, court and government seals, one quickly sees *numerous* tips of the hat that show us who pulls the strings of our nation and power. One does not have to be in government (necessarily) to control government - you just need to control the money. For now, it is sufficient to know that government, their policies and actions, are virtually entirely orchestrated for the consumption of the populaces. As the saying goes, "He who has the gold makes the rules." Always follow the money: who has it, what are they doing, what circles do they run in, and what are their intentions. If you want to know who really controls the world's strings, find out the occult-minded individuals that the nations borrow money from.

Planets appear as, and are also called, stars. The hexagram represents Molech/Chiun/Saturn - the sixth planet.

The swastika is a symbol with very ancient history, going back to the time of the Flood, and possibly before that. Generally, today, the left pointed version represents life, sun, power, strength and good luck. The Nazi use of it was from use in various occult orders (Teutonic Order, Thule Society, Vril Society). Hitler insisted that it always be shown pointing right (evil), and it's no accidental choice. It's Germanic sacred meaning was long associated with Nordic gods, Odin or Thor. At its core for many cultures, it is the sun. Hitler was a prototype of the final Antichrist; it should not surprise us that the occult played a very large, but clandestine, role with Hitler.

The Samarra Bowl (ca. 4000 BC) on exhibit at the Pergamon Museum, Berlin. From Samarra, Iraq, northern Mesopotamia. Note the sun god symbol in the center.

Solomon's Apostasy

When Solomon was old, his heart was turned to many false idols and the occult (I Kings 11). He ended up worshipping Chemosh, Molech, Ashtoreth (Queen of Heaven), and many other false gods (vs.7-8). Because of his involvement both with the Temple of the true God, and with so many false gods, he is often used in symbology and terms by occult and esoteric groups.

The Bible gives us a hint that Solomon's money and power is also (on top of marrying the heathen) what Satan eventually used as a means to get false worship into his life (I Kings 10:14); his love of money, power, and influence caused him to make alliances and unions with those God had clearly told him to stay away from. Satan still uses the same bait and hook today.

"But king Solomon loved many strange women, together with the daughter of Pharaoh, women of the Moabites, Ammonites, Edomites, Zidonians, and Hittites; of the nations concerning which the LORD said unto the children of Israel, Ye shall not go in to them, neither shall they come in unto you: for surely **they will turn away your heart after their gods:** *Solomon clave unto these in love."* - II Kings 11:1

Solomon's apostasy introduced a pantheon of false idols and gods into the Jewish lives and country - an influence that would cost them dearly. Not only did the king introduce such vile rituals and worship, but it was also adopted by the people as well. Eventually, many of these corruptions and influences formed the Jewish mysticism known as Cabbalism.

⛰ Babylonian Captivity

The tribes of Israel were taken into
Babylonian captivity for their years of idolatry
and worshipping false gods - and turning
their back on the true God; yet, in His mercy,
God told them they would return after 70 years.

Scripture repeatedly gives examples of God using pagan kings (Cyrus)
and nations (Babylon, Egypt, etc.) in times past. Even though Cyrus was
a pagan king, Isaiah 45:1 reads, *"Thus saith the LORD to his anointed,
to Cyrus, whose right hand I have holden, to subdue nations before him."*
Cyrus was a tool in God's hand. Also in Scripture, God points out that
sometimes He preserved and worked in a wicked and idolatrous Judah
solely for David's sake (I Kings 15:4) and the promises made to him.

Daniel & Babylon Captivity of Jews   ## Return from Captivity

70 yrs (Dan 9:2)

75-80+ YRS OLD

There were many old men who had
seen Solomon's Temple before
captivity, and witnessed both the
fulfillment of prophecy and the
rebuilding after captivity. Ezra 3:12.

Babylonian concepts started tainting Jewish oral law and teachings,
which were themselves much later codified in the Talmud
(vs Torah). It was during this exile time that the root of the mystical,
'New Age' Judaism, Kabbalism (Cabbalism) formed. Jewish-themed
magic and occultism. Also incorporated are the evolutionary cycle
ideals toward progress world unification, and integration of physical
and spiritual, under the lead of a messiah-like figure.

✝ Time of Christ

Jesus Christ, son of God, son of man, son of David
Matt 8:29, 17:22, Lk 1:32

Jesus was very harsh on the religious leaders of the Jews, and even some in the church, because He implied several times that they held (privately) to some esoteric and occult beliefs (Rev. 2:9,13: "synagogue of Satan"; Luke 11:19)

When Christ rose from the dead, and ascended to the Father, He also took with Him the dead in Christ (up till that point in history). *"When he ascended up on high, he led captivity captive..."* - Eph. 4:8.

*"In my Father's house are many mansions: if it were not so, I would have told you. I go to prepare a place for you. And if I go and prepare a place for you, **I will come again, and receive you unto myself; that where I am, there ye may be also.**"* - John 14:2-3.

Sometime before God sends judgment on the world (Tribulation), He will gather His faithful servants up to Heaven with Him **where He is now.** Seven years later, He will come down **with them** to defeat Satan, and reign **on Earth** for 1,000 years (Rev. 20).

Jesus Christ has no association with secret societies, and soundly condemned those involved with them (Ezek 8). He made it clear to the religious leaders that He always spoke openly and did not have secret sayings or doctrine (John 18:20). He also told His disciples *"Swear not at all..."* (Matt 5:34). James 5:12 also warns, *"But above all things, my brethren, **swear not, neither by heaven, neither by the earth, neither by any other oath...**"* Christians should have nothing to do with secret societies and their vile oaths.

⋈ The Early Church

The Church, the house (family) of God
Heb 3:6, I Pet 2:5

⋈

The true Church is not an organization, it is the family reunion of believers in Jesus Christ.

Paul warned the Galatians to not listen to any so-called angels who bring another gospel, or purported new revelation: Gal 1:8 - *"But though we, or an angel from heaven, preach any other gospel unto you than that which we have preached unto you, let him be accursed. "*

Sadly, many religious groups today have harkened to the things said by (fallen) angels rather than God, and even brand their literature as 'Another Gospel'.

Timothy was warned repeatedly by Paul to shun profane fables - stories utilizing pagan influences, characters, and means - all of which are often portrays as a moral story or lesson. Timothy, pastoring in idolatrous Ephesus, was warned not to be tempted with mixing pagan elements with true Gospel and faith - even for supposedly good causes. Even today, Satan deceives many Christians by using pagan elements, terms, etc. under the guise of moral lessons, so-called themes of redemption, etc. He also often portrays secret societies as beneficial or humanitarian in some regards to garner interest and whitewash the truth.

Jesus Christ made it clear that Mary was **not** extra special or divine:

Luke 11:27-28 - *"...a certain woman of the company lifted up her voice, and said unto him, Blessed is the womb that bare thee, and the paps which thou hast sucked. But he said, **Yea rather, blessed are they that hear the word of God, and keep it.**"*

I Timothy 2:5 - *"For there is one God, and **one mediator** between God and men, the **man Christ Jesus.**"*

The False Church

Catholicism is **the** pantheon of the world's false gods (including primarily Isis/Ishtar), deceptively renamed to appear of Christ. Many within and without are deceived. As a whole, it contains more idolatry than any other religion, with focus on Ishtar. The Vatican is **full** of graven images/icons. Whole books are written on this false church; we will hit only a few highlights.

The Catholic church subsumed much of the allegory and symbolism of the ancient esoteric mystery cults into its tenets.

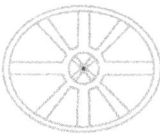

Baal, sun god

Ishtar, queen of heaven

Repackaged false gods

The largest Egyptian obelisk in existence is in the center of the plaza within a large sun wheel, symbolizing the union of male and female principles. Surrounded by pantheon of false gods. Easter (Ishtar)-related ceremonies take place here.

In the Vatican's Court of the Pine Cone, is the world's largest scuplted pinecone, with an empty sarcophagus before it. The pine cone has long been associated with the pagan gods, and their staffs are often adorned with them.It symbolizes fertility and opening the mind.

Lesser known by many, the Catholic church also has what are called Black Virgins. One is in the Vatican chapel used by Benedict and Francis. One of their striking features is that Mary is portrayed as masculine - because it is androgynous - man and woman. It is a beastly merging of Osiris, Horus, and Isis. Horus is Isis' son who sits on her lap.

Before their Babylonian captivity, the children of Israel were involved in worship of Tammuz (Eze 8:14), which corrolated to similar mythology.

"And they forsook the LORD, and served Baal and Ashtaroth." - Judges 2:13

"And he took away the horses that the kings of Judah had given to the sun, at the entering in of the house of the LORD, by the chamber of Nathanmelech the chamberlain, which was in the suburbs, and burned the chariots of the sun with fire." - II Kings 23:11.
The children of Judah had adopted some of the pagan sun worship, until Josiah burned them.

The Catholic church places the sun-god wheel above the heads of its 'saints', and calls it a halo. The statue of Peter inside the Vatican has a definite sun wheel above his head, and is thought to be Jupiter, of Roman Pantheon origin. The stylized sun and sunburst is also used throughout the Vatican's architecture and vestments.

The wafer represents the sun god who is reborn. The cross within the circle with the serpents head represents the sun god. During the Mass rituals, it is often placed in what is called a Monstrance, a sun burst for the audience to bow down and worship. Some often have a small cresent moon within to hold the wafer.

Religious Babylon (Rev. 17)
During the Tribulation, the Catholic Church, pantheon of false gods, will serve its purpose for a while, till religions are diluted and inter-faithed to unorthodoxy, experiences, and mysticism; it will then become disposable. This Religious Babylon is hated by the kings of the earth (Rev. 17:16) - but they will use it as long as it suits their purposes.

Jesus Christ made it clear that Mary was *not* extra special or divine:

Luke 11:27-28 - *"...a certain woman of the company lifted up her voice, and said unto him, Blessed is the womb that bare thee, and the paps which thou hast sucked. But he said, **Yea rather, blessed are they that hear the word of God, and keep it.**"*

I Timothy 2:5 - *"For there is one God, and **one mediator** between God and men, the **man Christ Jesus.**"*

God allows artistic expression, but forbids the worship of it.

The ark of the covenant had the cherubim on them, but they were only seen once a year, and nobody bowed down to them or prayed to them.

In the wilderness, the children were told to only look at the brazen serpent, not worship it (Num. 21:8-9). Later, it was destroyed because people did start worshipping and burning incense to it (II Kings 18:3-4).

Artistic depictions of oxen and angels, trees, etc. adorned the Temple, but they were never worshipped or venerated.

*"Thou shalt have no other gods before me. Thou shalt not make unto thee any graven image, or any likeness of any thing that is in heaven above, or that is in the earth beneath, or that is in the water under the earth: **Thou shalt not bow down thyself to them, nor serve them:** for I the LORD thy God am a jealous God, visiting the iniquity of the fathers upon the children unto the third and fourth generation of them that hate me."* - Exodus 20:3-5

The Tribulation First Half

Worship of the Queen of Heaven (under various titles) will probably become more overt, and used as a rallying point and 'common ground' for the various religions. The Catholics already refer to Mary as the Queen of Heaven [Pius XII encyclical, Ad Caeli Reginam].

In Islam, Mary (the Queen of Heaven) is revered as the True Sayyida, or Lady. Because the Catholic Mary has goddess qualities attributed to her, New Agers also have affinity for her.

The EU flag has 12 stars, inspired by the halo of twelve stars around pictures of Mary. Interestingly, the mythical Europa had the title "Queen of Heaven". Don't be surprised if, during the Tribulation, the EU flag is modified to have a more literal form of the queen of heaven.

Dilution & Unification
Phase

Many 'christians' &
'churches' in-name-only
will also transition.

THE WHORE
The Whore (Rev. 17) is the entity that pimps itself for the goal of unifying the world's religions.

Historic (Political & Commercial) Babylon Rebuilt (Rev. 18)

Apparently, during the Tribulation time, Babylon will be rebuilt for its original occult and pagan purposes. It will also be a hub of luxury and wealth; the kings of the earth love this Babylon. With the advancements of city building, especially by the Chinese, it is not a stretch to expect a modern city metropolis rising up, especially when Antichrist has spoiled and looted the previous religious Babylon. Along with the wealth will be the open practice of craft and all things forbidden by God (Deut. 18:9-12) - just like it was originally.

"...the habitation of devils, and the hold of every foul spirit, and a cage of every unclean and hateful bird. ...for by thy sorceries were all nations deceived."
- Rev. 18:1,23

"...I heard another voice from heaven, saying, Come out of her, my people, that ye be not partakers of her sins, and that ye receive not of her plagues." - Rev. 18:4

21

Satan's Chess Game

📖 *"...the devil said unto him,*
All this power will I give thee, and the glory of them:
for that is delivered unto me;
and to whomsoever I will I give it."
- Luke 4:6

LUCIFER

Satan has promised power, knowledge, skill, fame, and position to countless people down through the ages - all if they will bow down and worship him, and aid his iniquity.

*This illustration for concept purposes only, and does not represent any particular group or hierarchy.

📖 *"...Satan himself is transformed into an angel of light."*
- II Cor. 11:14

*"Judge not according to the **appearance,**
but judge **righteous judgment.**"*
- John 7:24

Clueless Pawns

There are millions of people involved in organizations, works, efforts, societies, etc. that have zero idea of what they are involved with. Many of them know only the superficial reasons given for their particular group or effort. Their effort, labor, finances, networking, etc. goes to support a cause they should have investigated further. Some organizations exist, (controlled by stakeholders), solely to create pressure in other areas. Even for secret societies, though, the initiates at this level will quickly start seeing symbols and vows that should raise serious red flags that they should leave.

Willful Pawns

As individuals stay in organizations (political, causes, religious, societies, orders, etc.) that are involved (minor or majors ways) in the mystery Babylon effort, they start attaining ranks, degrees, and some insider knowledge that all is not as it first appears. More and more involvement and advancement will weave them in. The fringe benefits of business and community networks (appeals to power and prominence) also help bind them from leaving.

Power Brokers

These are often emerging Strategic Players that start being groomed for future work and influence. By now, their involvement and knowledge, and participation in rituals and ceremonies also goes hand in hand with blackmail, stated or not. By now it is much harder to leave because of the powerful networks and occult forces woven into their lives.

Strategic Players

Many different levels, degrees, and statuses are covered in these tiers. Largely composed of those with financial power, means, religious sway, political capital, influences, etc. Many of these individuals have gotten to their higher places because of their insider connections. By this point they are more indoctrinated and initiated in some of the darker aspects, rituals, and ceremonies than the pawns have even thought of; in fact, many of the power brokers use their influence to disinform, manipulate, and deceive the pawns.

Royalty & Bloodlines

At the very top are very powerful individuals and families groomed, and selected from royalty to preserve the Satanic bloodlines through which the Antichrist will come. The general populace knows little or nothing of these genetic lines or efforts. The individuals and powerful families involved display double lives and loyalties. The depths of depravity and Satanic ritual abuse and sacrifice that they observe staggers the mind; yet, when we read of King Solomon getting involved with the royalty of the pagan Canaanite and Egyptian nations, the Bible clearly tells us that their occult worship brought him down to the place where even he worshipped Molech (Saturn) with human sacrifice (I Kings 11) - which expectably would have been his own children.

It is a bloodline and lineage to the Anunnaki (the seed of the serpent, Genesis 3:15) that the secret societies and luciferian groups actively promote and preserve. All occultic orders ultimately trace back to the annuaki, through Babylonian, Egyptian, and Sumerian roots.
The kings of this crossbreed succession were also known as 'Dragons'. Multiple kingdoms united selected one king: Great Dragon or Draco.

Satanic & Deceptive

The diabolical and horrendous ritualistic beliefs and actions of the Luciferians, Rosicrucians, and uppermost degrees in Freemasonry stagger the senses. Ritual abuse, sacrifice, sexual magic, etc. is routinely employed - it is the depths of the heart's iniquity. At the same time, these individuals can pass as cultured, upstanding families and men of society, who are often seemingly involved in many humanitarian efforts. Many appear to be Catholic, Protestant, or Marxist atheist. One late example is Josef Mengele, the Dr. Death of Auschwitz, who (years after the war) portrayed himself as a devout Christian - while still yet involved in devilish deeds. They have no moral compass whatsoever.

Decentralized?

There are many groups in the world that are started, funded, and steered by occult-minded individuals and families with great power; however, you cannot point to one or a few organizations - there are thousands of efforts, steered on various levels, with little or no knowledge of the ultimate purposes of their group or efforts. As progression, ranks, and degrees are attained in these groups, their occult knowledge and attachment is deepened.

Possessed Puppets

In Scripture, demon possession was not always overtly detectable (King Saul, Judas); likewise, today many have been initiated (willingly or forcefully) in rigorous rituals to place Satan's demons into their broken minds and lives to take control at key times (Mark 9:22). Many high-profile actors and musicians are prisoners and pawns in this category.

Religion

Satan, and his followers, know and study Scripture more than most Christians. Ever since the Garden of Eden, Satan has been twisting God's words for his own means. There are many religious organizations (of all stripes) and faith-based non-governmental entities that are employed in the mystery of iniquities efforts. Also, there are many religious leaders who are not what they appear to be, but are often involved with secret societies such as upper levels of Freemasonry. The Bible tells us that we are to try (righteously judge) the spirits, and examine one's spiritual fruits. Do not follow any religious leader who is involved in Freemasonry, especially if they are of several degrees - they are holding hands with the devil.

*"...**it is no great thing** if his ministers also be transformed as the ministers of righteousness; whose end shall be according to their works."* - II Cor. 11:15

*"...there shall be false teachers among you, who privily shall bring in damnable heresies, even denying the Lord that bought them, and bring upon themselves swift destruction. And many shall follow their pernicious ways; by reason of whom the way of truth shall be evil spoken of. And through covetousness shall they **with feigned words make merchandise of you...**"* - II Peter 2:1-3.

The Bible warns that there are individuals who will use stealth and deception **to use and exploit you** - your resources, affiliations, support, influence, etc. - all to profit their means, ends, and kingdom.

Don't forget that one of the first antichrist-types was Judas; he sang hymns, went on evangelistic trips, distributed to the poor, etc. - but Satan entered into this thief and phony (John 13:27). Even the disciples did not suspect him (13:29). Judas tracked and betrayed Jesus' whereabouts.

Positioning

Sometimes front groups, organizations, causes, etc. (with known connection to upper stakeholders) appear to be at conflict or opposition with other entities controlled by the same sources. However, many times this is done for problem/solution situations, controlling / leveraging resources, creating controlled division and chaos, or even just to occupy opposition energy and focus.

Everything is done for strategic purposes. When focusing on just the particular players, you may often not see the larger picture or game plan. This is also one major reason why there is a big focus on symbols - they represent which team one is on; other team players are recognizable, and go along with the show, even if there appears no logical or strategic connection.

Someone doesn't necessarily have to be boots-on-the-ground in an organization - they just have to be on the steering committees, founders club, sponsors group, board of directors, majority stockholder, etc. It is these who benefit from the sweat equity and synergy of the underlings.

The **mystery of iniquity** is not a single group, city, or organization - it is the Satanic occult campaign that has stayed behind the scenes, largely unrevealed, since the fall of man; but, it has been working fervently toward a final goal.

Not only is its goal Babylonianism
- to unify the world politically and economically -
but also to bring back the occult religions
of Babylon - with Satan at the forefront.

🕵️ Technology Role

Technology is a tool that can be used for bad or good. As Christians, we are called to *"...be ye therefore wise as serpents, and harmless as doves..."* (Matt 10:16).
As with anything that impacts us, or is woven into our lives, we must scrutinize its impact and potential misuse by our adversary - or our own flesh.

📖 *"Lest Satan should get an advantage of us: for we are not ignorant of his devices."* - Ephesians 2:2-3

Nazi Germany, especially toward the end of the war, made incredible strides in technology, in just a relative short time. Their stealth Horten bomber wing technology was **30 years more advanced** than what the Allied had. Other examples of the vast technology gap were their Messerschmitt jet and V2 rockets. It was all of this technology that America wanted - and worked into its own programs - regardless of the source and operators. **The occult source of much of their knowledge was also introduced** (Ahnenerbe). Credible evidence also suggests top Nazi scientists left Germany, via submarine convoys, prior to the war's end - with the best advancements, leaving lesser distractionary technology and scientists behind.

The first 'tabulating machine' (early computer) was developed by IBM and used by Hitler to greatly enable him to identify and classify millions of people for his devilish eugenic purposes. It is interesting to consider that the first computers (in a sense) became a beastly tool of Satan.

Data originating from you often says more about those with whom you are connected - and visa versa.

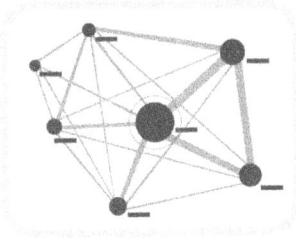

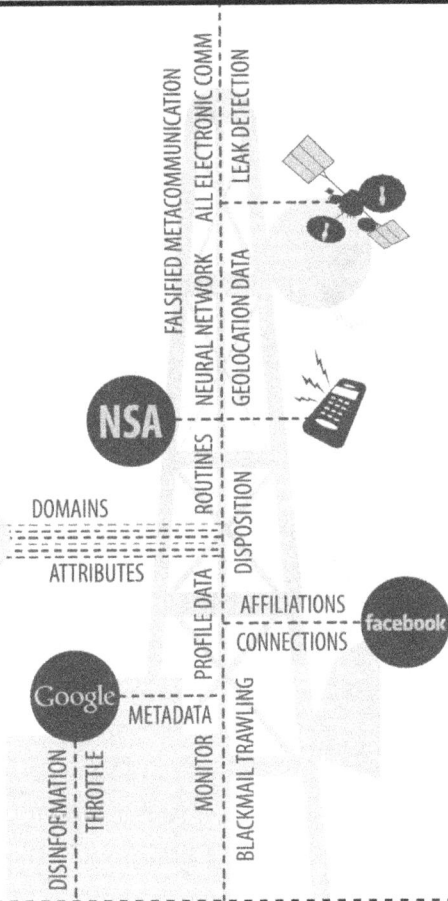

FALSIFIED METACOMMUNICATION
ALL ELECTRONIC COMM
LEAK DETECTION
NEURAL NETWORK
GEOLOCATION DATA
NSA
ROUTINES
DISPOSITION
DOMAINS
ATTRIBUTES
PROFILE DATA
AFFILIATIONS
facebook
CONNECTIONS
Google
METADATA
BLACKMAIL TRAWLING
DISINFORMATION
THROTTLE
MONITOR

TOP SECRET Once again, computer technology is used to gather information on those who are to be controlled - the citizens. The information gleaned is used for blackmail purposes, co-opting active participation by judges, politicians, military, and government leaders. This effectively neuters the governmental checks and balances. Those who hold the reins of power, finances, and information control the world's governments.

The controlled individuals continue to go through the motions, doing as they are instructed to do - leaving the populace to think their countries are run by idiots. The puppets will passionately champion and debate any cause - because they are told to. Judges in the highest courts of the land will not render true justice, and will turn a blind eye because they are blackmailed to. As the way Satan works, these individuals were given access to their carnal lusts - but they were all recorded.

Other dossiers are being compiled for future use as well. Your democracy in a republic is an illusion that vanished decades ago.

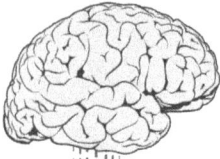

Your brain constantly processes and retains more visual information than your critical attentiveness catches; directors and media developers know this, and package information specifically to be retained and processed - without necessarily being attentively recognized. This is the main reason I do not have a television; even though, with my degree in Advertising and Public Relations, I can recognize many visual devices, I know I will not be able to see them all, sometimes even in hindsight. I know the power of media, and I don't want it used on me.

Many Christians have small sections in their house that are operated almost exclusively by foreign agents - foreign to this world, and foreign to Christian faith, doctrine, and godly living. Tribute and allegiance is usually given daily.

"...in time past ye walked according to the course of this world, according to *the prince of the power of the air,* the spirit that now worketh in the children of disobedience: Among whom also we all had our conversation in times past in the lusts of our flesh, fulfilling *the desires of the flesh and of the mind;* and were by nature the children of wrath, even as others."- Ephesians 2:2-3

TV & Media:
Programming & Conditioning
• Falsified Metacommunication
• Double Binds • Duplicity
• Cognitive Dissonance
• Exposure • Desensitization

Your brainwaves will naturally go into Alpha level thinking (vs Beta) while watching television - the best mode to receive these mental programming methods.

Media is carefully used to precondition populaces to mentally adopting actions, themes, ideas, and terms that will come into play later - it will also be used to distract you until then.

H.G. Wells' *War of the Worlds* radio broadcast was a social engineering test. It was performed on Halloween, Oct. 30, 1938.

The eye of Horus (sun god) motif so often seen actually maps and represents the controlling portions of your brain and mind. Satan wants your mind and thoughts, and he knows how to entertain you into retaining the way he wants you to think.

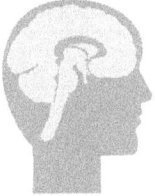

*"Judge not according to the **appearance,** but judge **righteous judgment.**"*
- John 7:24

HOLLYWOOD

Term derived from Druid's sacred fascination with the oak and holly, relating to the goddess of the underworld, Holle. Hollywood, thus is the place of magic in propaganda and conditioning.

The Hollywood & Highland Center, where the Oscar Awards are held (Kodak Theatre), has its own extra-large Ishtar-style gate, with four large reliefs of Babylonian Nusku and Assyrian Nisroch - one a fallen angel. They are so prominent, you can see them on Google Maps. Ishtar/Isis is also featured several times in the courtyard as well.

Of course, in line with the gate, across the street, is the old Freemasonry Temple, now owned and restored by Disney.

The whole gateway promenade visually centers and frames the Hollywood sign off on the hills in the distance.

Kinda, puts new perspectives on major features such as Star Wars (Anakin Skywalker and Luke Skywalker): a movie about rebelling and going to the dark side - or much more.

Every thing in major Hollywood productions is done on purpose.

🔭 Watching

✝ Israel Was Not Watching

The prophet Daniel had recorded in Scripture that from the time of the decree to rebuild Jerusalem, to the time of the Messiah, would be 69 sevened (times seven) - Dan 9:25. Israel was told to be expecting Messiah to be revealed 476 years after the walls were rebuilt - to the day!

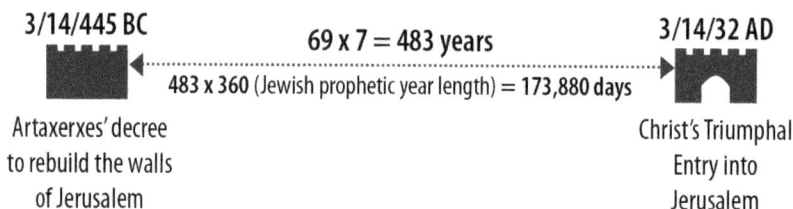

3/14/445 BC

69 x 7 = 483 years

483 x 360 (Jewish prophetic year length) = **173,880 days**

3/14/32 AD

Artaxerxes' decree
to rebuild the walls
of Jerusalem

Christ's Triumphal
Entry into
Jerusalem

**Jesus rode into Jerusalem on the very day He told them
He was going to, but they weren't watching for Him!**

---

*"...he beheld the city, and wept over it, saying, If thou hadst known, even thou, at least in **this thy day,** the things which belong unto thy peace! but now they are hid from thine eyes. For the days shall come upon thee, that thine enemies shall cast a trench about thee, and compass thee round, and keep thee in on every side, and shall lay thee even with the ground, and thy children within thee; and they shall not leave in thee one stone upon another; **because thou knewest not the time of thy visitation.**"* - Luke 19:41-44

For more in-depth study: Sir Robert Anderson's, *The Coming Prince.*

The prophet Ezekiel recorded God's promise that the nation of Israel would live again, using the picture of the valley of dry bones (Ezek. 37:1-14). As God showed Ezekiel, it would be a process coming together in stages, with the land refilling in stages, until His covenant is completely fulfilled.

The World Not Watching

While in the Babylon captivity, the prophet Ezekiel was told by God that Israel would bear the punishment (via dispersion) for their iniquity a total of 430 years (Ezek. 4:3-6). After the captivity ended, they still had 360 years left. After their freedom from captivity, though, they quickly returned to their ways of iniquity. In Leviticus 26, God warns four times that if Israel failed to hearken to God after His corrections, that He would multiply the punishments seven times more. The time remaining after their first chastening was 360 years.

Initial Dispersion Judgment:
430 yrs (Ezek. 4:3-6)

Extended Dispersion Judgment

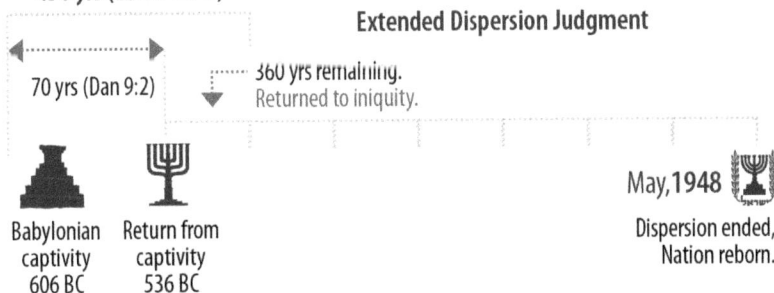

70 yrs (Dan 9:2)   360 yrs remaining.
                          Returned to iniquity.

May, 1948

Babylonian   Return from   Dispersion ended,
captivity   captivity   Nation reborn.
606 BC   536 BC

360 years x 7 (Lev. 26) = **2,520 prophetic years** (360 days)
2,520 prophetic years = **2,483.8 calendar years** (365 days)

Not only was it promised, but the nation of Israel was re-established right on time, according to the Scriptures.

Commanded To Watch and Be Vigilant

Throughout the New Testament, believers are to watch for His return, and to live in light of that event. Too many times, we get our eyes focused on this world, and it's kingdom, and we forget that we are to focus and live in light of eternity and Christ's kingdom.

*"**Watch** therefore: for ye know not what hour your Lord doth come."*
- Matthew 24:42

*"**Watch** therefore, for ye know neither the day nor the hour wherein the Son of man cometh."* - Matthew 25:13

*"Take ye heed, **watch and pray:** for ye know not when the time is. For the Son of man is as a man taking a far journey, who left his house, and gave authority to his servants, and to every man his work, and commanded the porter to watch. **Watch** ye therefore: for ye know not when the master of the house cometh, at even, or at midnight, or at the cockcrowing, or in the morning: Lest coming suddenly he find you sleeping. And what I say unto you I say unto all, **Watch.**"* - Mark 13:33-37

*"Blessed are **those servants,** whom the lord when he cometh **shall find watching:** verily I say unto you, that he shall gird himself, and make **them** to sit down to meat, and will come forth and serve **them.**"* - Luke 12:37.
Many Christians will be surprised that only those found watching (living and expecting) for His return will get the royal treatment.

*"Remember therefore how thou hast received and heard, and hold fast, and repent. If therefore thou shalt not **watch,** I will come on thee as a thief, and thou shalt not know what hour I will come upon thee."* - Matthew 25:13

*"Sell that ye have, and give alms; provide yourselves bags which wax not old, a treasure in the heavens that faileth not, where no thief approacheth, neither moth corrupteth. **For where your treasure is, there will your heart be also.**"* - Luke 12:33. Like Lot, those who invest their lives for earthly treasure and reputation will find that one day they will leave it all behind to be burned - they will leave empty handed.

*"The lord of that servant will come in a day when he looketh not for him, and at an hour when he is not aware, and will cut him in sunder, and **will appoint him his portion with the unbelievers.** And that servant, which knew his lord's will, and prepared not himself, neither did according to his will, shall be beaten with many stripes. But he that knew not, and did commit things worthy of stripes, shall be beaten with few stripes.*
For unto whomsoever much is given, of him shall be much required: *and to whom men have committed much, of him they will ask the more."*
- Luke 12:46-48. Those Christians who do not live in light of His return may find that their invitation to the wedding feast has been cancelled, and their appointment changed to stick it out on earth for seven years with the rest of the world who didn't live as though Christ would come one day.

I would rather have people say I search and watch too much, than for Christ to say I didn't watch at all.

---

*"Nevertheless we, according to his promise, **look** for new heavens and a new earth, wherein dwelleth righteousness. Wherefore, beloved, seeing that ye **look** for such things, be diligent that ye may be found of him **in peace, without spot, and blameless.**"* - II Peter 3:13-14

---

*"Beloved, now are we the sons of God, and it doth not yet appear what we shall be: but we know that, when he shall appear, we shall be like him; for we shall see him as he is. And **every man that hath this hope in him purifieth himself, even as he is pure.**"* - I John 3:2-3

The Last Generation

Jesus Christ told His disciples that all the end times events would occur within one generation's lifespan.

"Now learn a parable of the fig tree [Israel]; When his branch is yet tender, and putteth forth leaves, ye know that summer is nigh: so likewise ye, when ye shall see all these things, know that it is near, even at the doors."
- Matthew 24:32-33

He told them the start event which would mark the generation: the rebirth of Israel.

"The days of our years are threescore years and ten; and if by reason of strength they be fourscore years..."
- Psalm 90:10

The Bible tells us that an average lifespan is 70 years, and some average up to 80 years.

"This generation shall not pass, till all these things be fulfilled."
- Matt 24:34

Matthew 24:33 tells us, *"So likewise ye, when ye shall see all these things, know that it is near, even at the doors."* It implies that the generation referenced will already be old enough to see and remember the start event. For guesstimation's sake, 5 years old is safe enough to assume they can remember and make mental note of what happened.

Born

1943

Israel Re-Formed
May 15th, 1948

This Timeline is to get a sense of the generations since Israel's re-forming, as well as changes in our world that match, and fulfill, the prophecies regarding this final generation.

Background:

Modern era of passenger **airline service** begins in 1930s. Great aviation advances right after WW II, both in technology and use.

The Spanish Flu (1918-1919) is thought to be one of the most deadly pandemics in human history. This last generation would definitely know about it, and its impact on the world. Some may argue that AIDS has/will surpassed it.

World Wars Not The End - Many people around the world may have felt like the World Wars signaled the end of the world; but they, too, were also foretold that significant wars would precede the final signs: *"And ye shall hear of wars and rumours of wars: see that ye be not troubled: for all **these things must come to pass, but the end is not yet."*** - Matthew 24:6

Herd of Trojan Horses (1946)
Many Nazi scientists were brought to America at the end of the war (Operation Paperclip) under the banner that we needed their expertise. These quickly were given influential positions and access, often knowingly overlooking their pasts. Many of these war criminals were deeply involved in the occult. Their impact and influence, at these high levels, on the world's leading superpower is incalculable.

* The Baby Boomers were the first generation to think of generations as distinct; the accepted divisions between generations vary by several years according to researcher; recently the dates are more solidified.

"The Greatest Generation"

1940	
1941	• World War II (1939-1945) the most widespread war in history.
1942	
1943 — Born	
1944	• First rocket to reach space. A4 rocket, Wernher von Braun's team, Germany.

Baby Boomers - those born during this time that saw themselves as very different from previous. Grew up in time of dramatic social change. Greater propensitive toward social change. Peak levels of income. First generation heavily marketed to from birth to death. Global generation pattern, not just Americans. Often associated with counterculture, civil rights movement, and the feminist cause.

1945

1946 · Dr. Spock publishes his influential book on parenting. Later, *"The Spock Generation"* - a term referring to the two generations impacted by Dr. Spock's book. Characterized by instant gratification of needs, permissiveness, and narcissism.

1947

1948 — **5** YRS OLD   Israel Re-Formed May 15th, 1948

1949

Powerful political and financial influences and individuals involved with pushing certain goals, and making things happen, were the ones who insisted on the star symbol for the Israeli flag - contrary to those who wanted the menorah.

1950 · Korean War
· Color TV introduced in US

1951

1952

1953 — **10** YRS OLD · Queen Elizabeth II · Mt. Everest
· DNA discovered · Russia hydrogen bomb

1954 · Atomic submarine, Nautilus · School racial segregation banned

1955 · Churchill resigns · Rosa Parks

1956 · Egypt retakes Suez Canal · The US Interstate Highway System funded in 1956. The United States presently (2013) has the world's largest network of highways.

1957 · Sputnik launched

1958 · European Economic Community starts · Explorer 1, first US satellite
· Marines into Lebanon · China's Great Leap Forward Famine - the largest famine of all time.

1959 · Alaska & Hawaii become states · Castro takes over Cuba

1960 · Laser invented · U-2 spy plane shot down
· Adolf Eichmann captured in Argentina

1961 · First manned spaceflight · "information explosion" - term coined

1962 · US Supreme Court prohibits school-sponsored prayer
· Bullet trains start service · Mercury: (Odin), Atlas (king of Atlantis)

1963 — **20** YRS OLD

· Civil Rights Rally, MLK · JFK assassinated

1964 · Medicare begins

Generation X / MTV Generation - coined to describe the vast generational change from the previous generations. Raised by television like no previous generation. Also, the divorce rate (of their parents) skyrocketed during this period; reportedly also the worst divorces in American history; this fueled in their children what is often referred to as 'narcissistic wounds'.

1965
- Marines land in Dominican Republic • Gemini (king of the Underworld)

1966
- Hepatitis B discovered. Presently 350 million people are chronic carriers. 50-100Xs more infectious than HIV.

1967
- Six-Day War, Israel expands • China hydrogen bomb

1968
- N. Korea seizes Pueblo • MLK shot

1969
- Stonewall Riots marked open homosexual pride liberation movement
- Woodstock • ARPA goes online • U.S. moon program - Apollo (sun god)

1970
- US troops invade Cambodia • Jumbo Jet passenger airliners
- "information overload" coined • "data mining" becomes much more necessary • First Gay Pride marches: Los Angeles, Chicago, New York

1971

1972

1973 —
30 YRS OLD
- Roe v. Wade legalizes abortion • Watergate
- Yom Kippur War

1974

1975
- Pol Pot, Khmer Rouge, Cambodia • Apollo & Soyuz link

1976
- Supersonic passenger airliners, Concorde & Tupolev Tu-144
- US Bicentennial

1977
- Nuclear-proliferation pact signed • Jim Jones mass suicide

1978
- 1970-1990s - development and commercialization of Internet

1979
- Three Mile Island • Iran Revolution • Soviets invade Afghanistan

1980
- Iran-Iraq War

1981
- AIDS pandemic recognized • Pacman • Aspartame approved by FDA
- IBM introduces first PC • Israel annexes Golan Heights

Generation Y / Millennial Generation / Generation Me - noted and increased sense of entitlement and narcissism. Impacted heavily by technological developments. Also called **Trophy Kids** due to greater expectations of rewards. Also known as the **Boomerang Generation** or **Peter Pan Generation** due to delayed transition from childhood to responsible adulthood. Least religious generation, with greater trend toward irreligion (atheism, secular humanism, etc.).

1982  • Israel invades Lebanon • E.T. • Space Shuttle
 • Falklands War • First GMO plant for sale

1983 — **40 YRS OLD** • USC Declares many local abortion restrictions
 unconstitutional • Cell phone tests start • Cocaine

1984 enters US • US invades Grenada

 • Apple introduces Macintosh • Desktop publishing

1985

1986 • Chernobyl • Challenger explodes • Avg. household: 7hrs TV per day
 • Nintendo video games • USC Reaffirms abortion rights

1987 • 90% US homes have TV • Prozac released

1988 • RU486 permitted France, China
 • First WWW browser and server developed, Archie, WAIS

1989 • US invades Panama • Virtual Reality

1990 • Germany reunited • Kuwait invaded • X-rating replaced with NC-17
 • FDA approves implant contraceptive • Hubble Telescope

1991 • S.America Cholera epidemic • First TV condom ad • NAFTA
 • Soviet Union breaks up

1992  • USC reaffirms abortion rights • Rio Earth Summit
 50 YRS OLD • Los Angeles Riots • Maastricht Treaty, creating EU

1993 — • Homosexual military ban compromise • Waco

1994 • 1 million STD infections daily • Smartphones introduced
 • USC approves limits on abortion protests
 • Bosnia & Croatia • Chechnya

1995 • OK City Bombing • Cloning mainstreamed

1996 • Late-term abortion ban blocked • Ellen DeGeneres

1997 • Estimated new stored information doubled in three years
 • Heaven's Gate cult • Harry Potter

1998 • Euro agreed on • Kosovo • International Space Station

1999 • 150 million Internet users worldwide • Columbine

2000 • RU486 US approval • Human genome deciphered

2001 • Embyronic stell cell research • 9/11

2002

60
YRS OLD

• Increased travel has made possible the rapid spread of disease like never before.

2003

• Shuttle Columbia • Iraq War • Da Vinci Code

2004

• 1st US gay 'marriages' • SpaceShipOne

2005

• Gaza Strip handover • Terry Schiavo • 70 million web servers

2006

2007

• Apple's iphone introduced

2008

• 135 million web servers

While the Holocaust and Hitler's regime ended, the luciferian inflence found a new, eager home in America. The hidden influence would manifest itself over time in a new holocaust on our children, and steer our society away from God.

2009

• Swine Flu

2010

2011

2012

2013

70
YRS OLD

Israel's 65th Anniversary

2014

2015

2016

2017

2018

2019

2020

2021

80
YRS OLD
(POTENTIAL)

2022

2023

✅ Signs Fulfilled

🔑 Jesus Christ told His disciples that all the end times events would occur within one generation's lifespan.

"This generation shall not pass, till all these things be fulfilled." - Mt 24:34

Here is a list of events and signs (in no particular order) that will describe and occur within the last generation timeframe.

Diverse Earthquakes (Matt. 24:7) – Awareness sign. Note that the Scripture verse contains the qualifier, *"in divers places."* The point that it is making is not necessarily that earthquakes will increase, but that you will finally get to a period in time where you can be made readily aware that earthquakes are happening all over the world, and sometimes in some pretty remote places. Consider that we now also have the ability to record and monitor earthquakes that happen on land, and deep underwater, too - with pinpoint accuracy.

Religious Persecution (Matt. 24:9) – There is more persecution of Christians going on in our time and generations than at any point in history before. The intense persecution in Islamic countries, harsh crackdowns in Communist countries, and even subtler forms of persecution in countries which have other religions as their dominant religion. Sadly, much persecution escapes the attention of Christians in affluent countries. Even secular sources will confirm that the majority of Christians killed by persecution has been greatest in the twentieth century and onward.

Famines (Matt. 24:7) – The devastation and aftermath of World War II triggered numerous famines in the years after the war. Widespread famines in Africa and even incredible modern day shortages affect varying areas of the world. With this, the world is also experiencing records droughts and wildfires.

Tribal and National Wars (Matt. 24:7)
We have seen a wide variety of ethnic-related wars, wars of aggression, wars for political gain and posturing, as well as civil wars. Also, the average person around the globe is aware of minute real-time information, pictures, and video in many ways regarding these ongoing, and sometimes isolated, wars.

Marked Transportation Growth (Daniel 12:4)

Israel Re-established
(Isaiah 66:7-8; Zec. 12:1-6; Matt. 24:32-35)

Regathering of the Jews Begins
(Isaiah 11:10-12)

World politics focus on Israel
(Zechariah 12:3)

Revival of Biblical Hebrew language (Zephaniah 3:9; Jeremiah 31:23)
It was largely replaced with Aramaic after Jerusalem destruction.

Resurgence of Israeli military
(Zechariah 12:6)

Land of Israel flourishes
(Ezekiel 36:34-35; Isaiah 35:1-2,7)

Re-occupation of Jerusalem
(Luke 21:24, Zechariah 12:3)

Righteous Despised (II Tim. 3:3)
When a society and world gets to where they are proud and boastful of their sins, they will also despise and loathe any who would like godly or moral. It is ironic that the ones who call for 'tolerance' of their sin are the most intolerant.

False Christs (Matt. 24:5,23-24)
With the increase of internet and television media, we are definitely seeing more of these come out of the woodwork as they can easily pander to a fawning crowd.

Proud Boasters (II Tim. 3:2)

Not only is our society and world more sinful today, but they have no problem boasting about their sin and taking pride in what is wrong. Most people do not blush any more at sin, but wear it as a badge. Large segments of sinful behavior have even taken the title and banner of pride.

Materialistic (II Tim. 3:2) – Vast segments of our world are in deep debt because of their hunger and pursuit after things of this passing world. Whether it is cars, homes, or electronic gadgets, the things of this world have captivated their fancy, and large segments of our commerce and world economy is situated to appease their every whim. Sadly, a large portion of marketing is toward Gen X who never had the childhood of the 50s.

Hard Hearted (II Tim. 3:3)

"Without natural affection..." When a society's conscience is so seared by sin, narcissism, headonism, and paganism, it will naturally follow that the innate love and compassion toward others will be hardened and calloused. True love will be replaced with lusts, selfish control, narcissism, and other forms.

Traitors/Betrayers (II Tim. 3:4)

With narcissism (self-love) and a general hardening, many people today do not think much of climbing over one another, stabbing them in the back, or shoving someone under the proverbial bus.
The materialistic and selfish individual goals are more important to them than anything else. You will also find many media shows today promote this sense of betrayal for the individual or group good.

Disobedient to Parents (II Tim. 3:2)

This one is so obvious and glaring that even the secular world sees it. Many grandparents and older adults remark that if they acted like some bratty and smart-mouthed kid they saw at the store their parents would have fixed the situation post haste. Today's children are spoiled rotten with little true respect for authority or parents. It shouldn't surprise us that a large segment of our youth are on various medications to make them 'more controllable'.

Heady/Rash (II Tim. 3:4)

We find that people today are much more impulsive, hasty thinkers, and jumping to actions and conclusions with passion, but without much thought. This could be attributed in part to the bombardment of mental judgment and a shortened attention span from copious media consumption. It also comes from a society that is taught in general to not consider the consequences often, but taught to live in the moment.

False Accusers (II Tim. 3:3)

The propensity to lie and slander, notably under court oath, is becoming frequent enough to be commonplace.

Blasphemers (II Tim. 3:2)

Not only is God's name, and all things holy, profaned in every concourse, but it is also pumped into home via visual and audio educational means - commonly called the media. It would be a shock to most of society if a mainstream movie was made without profanity or cursing now a days.

Hardening, Lack of Love (Matt 24:12) -

"...because iniquity shall abound, the love of many shall wax cold."
People will become so inured and deadened through sin that most people will have little or no true love and compassion. There will be a hardening. Some of this is attributable to the media and movies which have desensitized people to a wide range of emotions - including true love.

Unthankful (II Tim. 3:2)

When a generation is taught that life revolves around them, and that pleasures and things are ultimately for their enjoyment, then we should not be surprised that a deep sense of entitlement, loss of work ethic, and demands for their every whim characterize so many young people and adults these days. There is no sense of being thankful for it beyond mere lip service. This characteristic is more commonly seen in affluent countries and societies, yet it is a unique trait to recent generations. Never before have large portions of mankind been so pampered and spoiled.

Pestilences (Matt. 24:7)

Many False Prophets (Matt. 24:11)
You can find a guru or self-proclaimed prophet touting themselves to be somebody in almost every city. Healers and such can draw a crowd, but even the Bible records false prophets who did the same. Today, though, you don't have to go far to find them. Most city newspaper classifieds are filled with purported healers and shamans who use everything except true Christianity and Jesus Christ.

Without Self Control (II Tim. 3:3)
When a society and generation is taught to follow their heart and emotions, over sound judgment and logic, we should not be surprised to see little regard to consequences of poor decisions. We see this largely in the form of debt, sexual diseases, divorce, errors in faith, etc. Because these individuals focus on themselves and their wants and desires, it is often hard to convince them otherwise, even though you could show they are making unwise choices.

Profane / Unholy (II Tim. 3:2)
As more and more people turn their back on God, we are finding a large surge in those who profess atheism and agnosticism. We are also seeing a growing number of people turning to witchcraft, Wicca, Satanism, and other pagan forms.

Trucebreakers (II Tim. 3:3)
Honest and truthful people are very, very hard to find. Your great-grandparents (and forefathers) lived in a time where a man's word was his bond; not so in this generation.

Hedonistic (II Tim. 3:4)
Society worldwide is in large pursuit of toys and pleasures. Things and pursuits of lasting value are scorned in exchange for living in the moment, regardless of the consequences.

Notable Growth in Knowledge (Daniel 12:4)

Signs in the Moon (Luke 21:25)

Awareness sign. Not yet seen. This may be more evident during the Tribulation, as implied in Mark 13:24, "...after that tribulation, the sun shall be darkened, and the moon shall not give her light..." In context (Rev. 6:12), it appears that the dust kicked up by the large, great earthquake will turn the moon a blood red. What is happening to Earth will be reflected in a visible way to all mankind by the effect it has on the moon in the sky.

Fierce/Savage (II Tim. 3:3)

Sadly, the brutal and savage acts of barbarianism reported in the news are becoming more commonplace. It is becoming commonplace to hear of parents slaying their own children, gunmen trying to kill as many as they can, torture, brutal sexual assaults, kidnapping, etc. Many of these horrific crimes would have been rarely heard of fifty years ago; yet, you can almost not go a day without hearing multiple cases of such in our times.

Narcissism (self-love) (II Tim. 3:2) – When a society is taught that life

is about them, and their pleasures are the only thing that matter, we should not be surprised that overwhelming segments of our society today cannot relate to others; they are totally self-absorbed in their own world and desires.

Global Video Communication (Revelation 11:8-9)

Europe Begins to Reunify (EU) - (Daniel 2:41-44, 7:8, 24-25)

False Godliness (II Tim. 3:5)

Sadly, one of the signs is the prevalence of a false sign: people pretending to be godly and Christian, yet just going through the motions. The passage tells us that while they have a form of godliness, they also deny "the power thereof..." In other words, they want to appear spiritual, 'Christian', etc. but they do not want God in their life or to tell them what to do. All around our nation and world we see 'churches' preaching everything but a call to repentance and godly living. There is no fear of God in them.

Signs in the Stars (Luke 21:25) – Awareness sign. Just within the past decades have we really become aware of the near-earth flybys and news of celestial note that we were largely unaware of a generation ago. We are now also seeing and able to see (through mass media and internet) fireballs and meteorite strikes - events that up till recently were seen by only a few at a time. These signs will continue through the Tribulation period as well.

Signs in the Sun (Luke 21:25) – Awareness sign. Only in the last decade or so have we not only gained a much clearer and ongoing picture of solar activity, but we can now watch it in high-definition in real-time (SOHO, IRIS satellites, etc.). We also have a much clearer understanding of significant solar events such as solar flares, coronal mass ejections, etc.

"So likewise ye, when ye shall see all these things, know that it is near, even at the doors.
This generation shall not pass,
till all these things be fulfilled."
- Matt 24:33-34

⬤⬤ Days of Noah & Lot

> **Jesus said the last days would be as the days of Noah and Lot:**
>
> *"...as it was in the days of Noe, so shall it be also in the days of the Son of man. ...Likewise also as it was in the days of Lot..."* - Luke 17:26,28

Pre-Flood Generations Timeline:

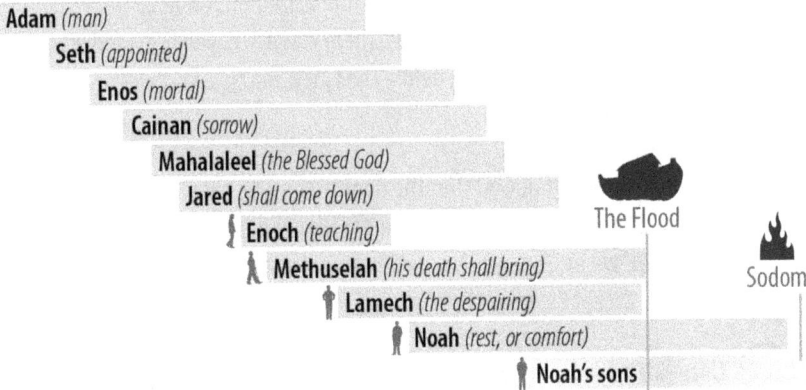

Adam *(man)*
Seth *(appointed)*
Enos *(mortal)*
Cainan *(sorrow)*
Mahalaleel *(the Blessed God)*
Jared *(shall come down)*
Enoch *(teaching)*
Methuselah *(his death shall bring)*
Lamech *(the despairing)*
Noah *(rest, or comfort)*
Noah's sons

The Flood

Sodom

ℹ️ Enoch

Noah's great grandfather, is the first recorded prophet; he told of Christ's second coming and judgment (Jude 1:14-15). Enoch is also the first person (of two) who was called up to Heaven without dying (Gen. 5:24).

🔑 Methuselah

Noah's grandfather. The name Methuselah comes from two roots: *muth* ("death") and *shalach*, ("to bring," or "to send forth"); thus, the name Methuselah signifies, "his death shall bring." He was the longest living human: 969 years. He died right before the Flood. It was understood by five generations that judgment was coming after he died; the world was warned that the Flood was coming.

Noah was told exactly how long the timeframe would be until the **Flood prophecy was fulfilled.**

•••••••••••••••••••➤
120 yrs (Gen 6:3)

Noah

In Genesis 7:1, God also references Noah in relation to his generation: *"Come thou and all thy house into the ark; for thee have I seen righteous before me in this generation."* Adam and Seth were dead, Enoch gone (Gen. 5:24); apparently, Methuselah also had just finally died.

God called Noah and his family to safety in the Ark **before** He sent judgment upon the world; likewise, just like Noah and the animals were gathered onto the ark, God will call His children home **before** He judges the world with the Tribulation; Jesus emphasized this point to His disciples (Luke 17:27). Interestingly, there was a 7-day wait period after God called them into the Ark before the Flood waters completely destroyed the world (Gen. 7:10).

The Bible tells us that God shut the door to the Ark, not Noah (Gen. 7:16). Only God knows when it will be time for His children to be called home; until then, we must stay busy making sure we are ready, and calling on others to accept Christ as their Saviour, too.

Once Noah, his family, and the animals were called into the safety of the ark it was too late for them to make life changes, or set things right - all of that had to be done before the call. They had to make sure they were prepared for the other side before they got on the Ark; likewise, for us, only one life will soon be past, only what's done for Christ will last.

While Noah did not control the 'when', there was a window in the ark (Genesis 6:16). Noah also had the prophetic life of Methuselah. There were ways for him to glimpse the signs of the times; likewise, God has given us over forty signs that we see being fulfilled within the timeframe that He has told us of.

Interestingly, Noah was still alive for the early portion of Lot's life.

God made sure Lot and his family were taken to safety **before** He sent judgment on Sodom (Luke 17:29); Jesus here emphasized this point to His disciples.

🛢 Middle East Wars

ISRAEL: Victory, Prosperity, Deception, & War

Psalm 83 describes a local confederacy of Israel's immediate neighbors that moves against Israel some time after it has been re-established. According to Psalm 83, the goal will be to completely erase Israel and create a new Palestine state. This may happen around the beginning of the Tribulation, and may be the event that necessitates the signing of a covenant with Israel (Dan. 9:27).

TURKEY

CYPRUS

SYRIA

LEBANON

Beirut☆ ☆Damascus

ISRAEL

Jerusalem ☆ ☆Amman

IRAQ ☆

JORDAN

EGYPT

Red Sea

SAUDI ARABIA ☆

●Mecca

✳ The Bible references these by people groups and geographic areas, not necessarily by today's borders - but still predominately the same parties.

Syria may be the linchpin, since it commands allies in Hezbollah, Hamas, and Iran. If Syria launches an attack on Israel, others may join in. The neighbors may attack in unison against their common enemy. Might be triggered by Israeli attack on Iran facilities.

Isaiah 17 tells that Damascus (capital of Syria) will be destroyed down to rubble in less than a day. The description implies nuclear destruction. Syria may be now on the threshold of triggering these events. Such drastic action against the city may also dissuade Iran and others from also getting involved and attacking.

These events will disrupt the Suez Canal, seriously disrupting oil shipments, commerce, and the ability for navies to navigate through there. It would possibly also shut down oil production in the region. The global domino effects will be incredible. Instant gas shortages (by real or rumored causes). Some regions may implement scorched-earth policies when they see they are losing.

This victory would most likely involve the destruction of Islam's two holiest sites - the Dome of the Rock and Mecca. The resulting psychological impact for its followers around the world would be devastating as they see their moon god is powerless. If this regional war takes place just prior to the beginning of the Tribulation, this would open the door for the rebuilding of the Temple, and the covenant brokered by the Antichrist with Israel's enemies.

Ezekiel 28:25-26 tells us that the judgment on those around Israel will be total and complete.

Psalm 83 implies that this confederacy will be completely destroyed and taken over for spoil. The armament, wealth, Infrastructure, mineral and oil resources, etc. will definitely make Israel a power to be reckoned with. It will also probably give Israel control over the Red Sea and partial control over the Strait of Hormuz - through which a large portion of oil trade flows. It also gives Israel control of the 'Crossroad of the World."

This event will completely overturn the oil cartel, influence, etc. It will also cut off the main funders of Islamic works and terrorist activity around the globe. Be ready for social chaos as various people lose all they had their faith in (financially and religiously). There may be local acts of revenge and retaliation in other nations.

Due to the rapid development of events, the US involvement will likely be limited to missile shipments and resupply.

EGYPT: Civil War & Drying of Nile

📖 ISAIAH 19:1-25

V.2 - Civil warfare will erupt, likely political and sectarian division. This will spiral out of control: first cities, then with spillover into regional conflicts.

V.4 - After a period of war, it appears that the Antichrist will eventually subjugate Egypt (Daniel 11:40-45). This could also refer to an intermediate dictator that deals harshly during this time of civil war.

"the river shall be wasted and dried up." vs.5-10. This appears to be the result of abnormal events disrupting the water flows, not related to normal dam construction. Apparently, any industry (fishing, agricultural, textile, industrial, etc.) and economic enterprises related to the river (and perhaps the Suez Canal) will be ruined because of the disruption. Complete economic and industrial collapse.

Egypt, which is already dependant on foreign aid, will self-destruct economically when its water resources are gone. Egypt depends entirely on the Nile for irrigation. The Aswan High Dam currently regulates the Nile and created a fishing and factory industry in Lake Nasser. It also provides around 15% of Egypt's electricity. Most of the water released by the dam is diverted to irrigation canals.

V.10 indicates that perhaps the dam and irrigation works are targeted and destroyed. This may be in regards to military retaliation.

IF Egypt attacks Israel in some form or fashion, Israel may find it easiest to just knock these dams out of commission, effectively cutting Egypt's power off at the knees and redirecting their armed forces focus toward civilian and situation control.

V.17 - Apparently, part of the regional spillover results in conflicts with Israel - to which Israel retaliates with crushing force. The Egyptians have already witnessed in recent past history how Israel has defeated them, and they know they are no match. This verse implies that a large part of the terror upon Egypt is a result of Israel's retaliation. Perhaps part of it involves the bombings of the Aswan Dams.

V.18 - the regional conflict will result in Israel capturing more territory. One city appears to have been the site of particular devastating attack during the conflicts.

Blood Moons

The celestial event grouping (four Blood Moons with no intervening partial lunar eclipses is called a **Lunar Tetrad**) with a Total Solar Eclipse (March 20, 2015) in the middle, appears to be very notable signs in the heavens.

The four Blood Moons (reddish from Earth partially blocking Sun's light) all occur on Jewish holy days (rabbinical calendar), Passover and Sukkot (Feast of Tabernacles). The last Tetrads occurred at the end of WWII (1949/1950) and the Arab-Israeli 6-Day War (1967/1968).

This will not repeat for again till distant future. Just like the previous two Tetrads, this one appears to mark a significant time for Israel. Of the three Tetrads: the first one seems to have signaled Israel's **return to the land;** the second, Israel's **return of Jerusalem;** the third, *possibly* the **return of the Temple mount.**

[● ● ● ● 1949-1950 (first in over 300 years)]

[● ● ● ● 1967-1968]

[● ● ● ● ● 2014-2015]

| April 15th | October 8th | Total solar eclipse March 20th | April 4th | Sept 28th (super moon) |

With the multiple significant celestial signs that point to the April 2014 timeframe, it is not a stretch to conclude that significant prophetic world-changing geopolitical events will be be transpiring that may forever alter the course of world events.

☪ Islam's Role

Since their respective starts, Islam and Catholicism have both become two of the dominant religions, with Islam recently taking the lead, and the esoteric lately gaining more *visible* ground and popularity...

Islam not final religion?

Different views think that Islam will be the one-world religion of the final days. However, Scripture shows that the occult and mystery religions will prevail, with Satan finally demanding full focus. When we look at the power brokers today, and that their money, influence, and occult desire is toward efforts and organizations, means, etc. toward Jewish and Israel ends - to ultimately accomplish their goals. Little of their focus is toward Muslim means - except to maintain and steer regional frictions. Islam, and Muslim power, is too fractured and divisive to wield its potential - and these fractures are what are continually fomented and stirred exactly for that reason.

Islam's Collapse?

It appears that the near concurrent fulfillment of Biblical prophecies regarding Syria, Israel, Egypt, and immediate regional countries, deals a large and swift death blow to the god of Islam. Its followers are melded into the emerging unified faith by their strong reverence toward veneration of Mary (Lady of Fatima), largely identical to Catholic positions. With their main god shown to be false, they may then switch to the remaining alternative pagan godess.

"...let every man take heed how he buildeth thereupon. For other foundation can no man lay than that is laid, which is Jesus Christ. Now if any man build upon this foundation gold**, silver, precious stones, wood,** hay**, stubble;** *Every man's work shall be made manifest: for the day shall declare it, because it shall be revealed by fire; and* **the fire shall try every man's work of what sort it is.** *If any man's work abide which he hath built thereupon, he shall receive a reward. If any man's work shall be burned, he shall suffer loss: but he himself shall be saved; yet so as by fire."* - I Cor. 3:10-15

Your Book of Works

= 👑 **Rewards for Service** (gain or loss) I Cor. 3:13-15

There will still be nations and positions for the saints rewarded. Some of God's children, who lived only for the former world, will have nothing (I Cor. 3:15).

THE HIGHEST HONOUR

*"...**Well done, thou good and faithful servant:** thou hast been faithful over a few things, I will make thee ruler over many things: enter thou into **the joy of thy lord.**"*

Matthew 25:21

WELL FAITHFUL SERVANT DONE

*"...every man that striveth for the mastery is temperate in all things. Now they do it to obtain a corruptible crown; but we an **incorruptible.**"* - Matthew 25:21

*"I have fought a good fight, I have finished my course, I have kept the faith: Henceforth there is laid up for me a **crown of righteousness,** which the Lord, the righteous judge, shall give me at that day: and not to me only, but unto all them also that love his appearing."* - II Timothy 4:7-8

*"Blessed is the man that endureth temptation: for when he is tried, he shall receive the **crown of life,** which the Lord hath promised to them that love him."* - James 1:12

*"when the chief Shepherd shall appear, ye shall receive a **crown of glory** that fadeth not away."* - I Peter 5:4

Showcase of Special Honor

"...a book of remembrance was written before him for them that feared the LORD, and that thought upon his name. And they shall be mine, saith the LORD of hosts, in that day when I make up my jewels..."
- Malachi 3:16-17

"And they that be wise shall shine as the brightness of the firmament; and they that turn many to righteousness as the stars for ever and ever." - Daniel 11:32-35

Tribulation Time & Dates

This chart, and all accompanying research, goes under the premise that it **appears** the second week in April will mark the Tribulation start, based on the celestial events in 2017. Corresponding prophetic events are listed and proposed accordingly, but it is still **conjecture.**

Season of Christ's Gathering His Church

Tribulation Start?
Apr 12, 2014   1,260 days prior to midpoint event (Rev. 11:3)

Tribulation Midpoint?
Sept 23, 2017

2014   2015   2016   2017   2018   2019   2020   2021

1,260 days will be after midpoint event (Rev. 12:6)   **Mar 6, 2021**
Tribulation End?

"And from the time that the daily sacrifice shall be taken away, and the abomination that maketh desolate set up, there shall be a thousand two hundred and ninety days. Blessed is he that waiteth, and cometh to the thousand three hundred and five and thirty days." (Daniel 12:11).
IF Sept. 23, 2017 is the day the desolation is set up,
then 1290 days later would be Apr. 5th, 2021.
1335 days from Sept. 23, 2017 would be May 20th, 2021.

The generation that was 5 years old when Israel was re-formed would potentially reach 80 years old in 2023 - the cap of an 80 year average lifespan (Psa 90:10). The Tribulation fits perfectly within the generation timeframe that Christ said it would (Matt 23:32-34).

80
YRS OLD
(POTENTIAL)
2023

The Book of Revelation

Understanding Revelation
Since Revelation is the last book given, it assumes you are familiar with the other books that Christ has given and stated beforehand; therefore, you must consider the other passages and context of the Bible when interpreting Revelation. If you attempt to interpret this book by *"private interpretation"* (by itself, II Peter 1:20), you will come to wrong conclusions. Always compare scripture with scripture, and consider the whole.

Understanding *when* things happen, *where* things happen, *who* is involved, and *how* things happen is vital to properly understanding prophecy.

The Book of Revelation is Chronological
"...Write the things which thou hast seen, and the things which are, and the things which shall be hereafter." - Rev. 1:19

The 7-Year Tribulation Period

Present Day　　　**Midpoint**
(both of the book, and the Tribulation)　　　**Conclusion**

Terrible Symbols
One reason Revelation uses symbols is because many of the things that John is describing beggar the imagination in adequately being able to describe the terrible awfulness of death and destruction that will be common and prevalent during this time of Tribulation. Even Christ, Himself, remarked that if He didn't limit to only seven years that all of mankind would be destroyed. Only a fraction of humanity will be alive when Christ finally returns; He is shattering the world's rebellion against Him with a rod of iron (Psalm 2:9). The entire world will essentially be a wilderness of ruin and destruction as a result of its rebellion when Christ comes back (Isaiah 14:16-17).

The Seven Churches

The Apostle John, on Earth, recorded Christ's warnings to the seven Churches that He was coming quickly, and that most of them needed to repent because He was coming quickly (Rev. 2:5,16; 2:21-22; 3:3).

Christ wanted all seven letters in one book distributed to all of the churches. It was a guide that all Christians can take note from. The churches were represented by candlesticks. 'Church' is only a collective term refering to an assembled group of Christians. Christians are called lights. When we get together, we have a candlestick. The 'church' is not an organization. When Christ refers to the church, He is referring to people, not organizations.

Notice that the rewards that He promises are two things: literal rewards such as a crown or position; and pictures of a restored relationship and fellowship with Him. Sin in our life blocks fellowship. Christ desires our fellowship and communion with Him more than anything else.

Notice that the negatives Christ is offended by the most is when Christians just go through the motions or play 'church'. If your name was placed instead of one of the churches, what would God praise and caution you about?

Ephesus

POSITIVES	NEGATIVES	CAUTION	REWARD
• Faithful • Active, busy • Hated deeds of Nicolaitanes (false teachers)	• Left their first love, Jesus Christ.	• Return unto first love or be removed	• Eat of the Tree of Life

John, on Earth

Smyrna

POSITIVES	NEGATIVES	CAUTION	REWARD
• Persecuted • Poverty	• None mentioned	• Be faithful unto death	• Receive a crown of life

Pergamos

This city was the location of Satan's altar (Zeus' temple) and seat of power. Rev. 2:13

POSITIVES	NEGATIVES	CAUTION	REWARD
• Faithful • Antipas, martyr	• Doctrine of Balaam • Doctrine of Nicolaitanes	• Repent	• Eat of the hidden manna • Given a white stone with a new name

Thyatira

POSITIVES	NEGATIVES	CAUTION	REWARD
• Active	• A Jezebel, teaching idolatry	• Repent • Hold fast till He comes	• Give power over the nations • Be given the morning star, Christ. Rev. 22:16 [close fellowship]

Sardis

POSITIVES	NEGATIVES	CAUTION	REWARD
• None mentioned	• Name that thou livest, but art dead	• Hold fast to what was received, and repent • He will come as a thief	• Clothed in white raiment

Philadelphia

POSITIVES	NEGATIVES	CAUTION	REWARD
• Kept my word, not denied my name	• None mentioned	• Persecution is coming • Deliverance because of faithfulness • I come quickly, hold fast to thy crown	• Pillar in the temple of my God • Inscription

Laodicea

• The city was known for a special eye ointment, and it's lukewarm water.

POSITIVES	NEGATIVES	CAUTION	REWARD
• Neither cold nor hot, lukewarm		• I will spue thee out • Be zealous and repent • Rebuke and chastening coming • Buy of Him gold, raiment, eyesalve	• Come in and sup with you • Sit with me in my throne

🕎 The Church In Heaven

📖 *"After this* ...*I heard was* **as it were** *of a trumpet talking with me; which said,* **Come up hither,** *and I will shew thee things which must* **be hereafter.**"* - Rev. 4:1

This chapter marks the transition from the church to the world. Christ's gathering of the church happens before the Tribulation. Christ had John write the events that come before and after the church period, and even used the same imagery to reinforce the transition. Prior to chapter 4, the church is mentioned as in the world 19 times; now that the church is in Heaven, it is no longer mentioned in the book of Revelation as being in the world. However, when we get to chapter 4, we find that the church is still the subject of discussion, but that it is in Heaven! The very first verse in chapter four emphasizes *twice* that this event of the church in Heaven comes immediately after the church period on earth - but before the Tribulation even starts.

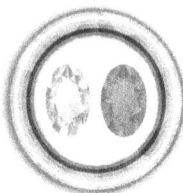

"...and, behold, a throne was set in heaven, and one sat on the throne. And he that sat was to look upon like a jasper and a sardine stone: and there was a rainbow round about the throne, in sight like unto an emerald." - Rev. 4:2-3
[FYI, rainbows really are round, when viewed from space]

The rainbow is a beautiful picture of God's covenant never to flood the entire earth again (Gen. 9:11-17). In the midst of all the Tribulation judgments about to be poured out, a global flood is not one of them. *"...in wrath remember mercy."* - Hab. 3:2

The jasper (purple/diamond) perhaps refers to the jasper on the High Priest's breastplate that signified Benjamin - "the son of my right hand". Sardis, a bright red, perhaps refers to the stone that represented Reuben - the firstborn of Jacob. Jesus Christ is the firstborn from the dead, the Son of God, who sits on the right hand of God the Father.

🌥 John In Heaven

"And round about the throne were four and twenty seats: and upon the seats I saw four and twenty elders sitting, clothed in white raiment; and they had on their heads crowns of gold." - Rev. 4:4

These elders represent the church (Titus 1:5). They are now in Heaven, wearing their robes of redemption, and wearing the crowns that were promised to them when He returned (Rev. 22:12).

- -

*"...and in the midst of the throne, and round about the throne, were four beasts full of eyes before and behind. And the first beast was **like** a lion, and the second beast **like** a calf, and the third beast had a face **as** a man, and the fourth beast was **like** a flying eagle. And the four beasts had each of them six wings about him; and they were full of eyes within: and they rest not day and night, saying,*

Holy, holy, holy, Lord God Almighty, which was, and is, and is to come."
- Rev. 4:6-8

"The four and twenty elders fall down before him that sat on the throne, and worship him that liveth for ever and ever, and cast their crowns before the throne, saying...

Thou art worthy, O Lord, to receive glory and honour and power: for thou hast created all things, and for thy pleasure they are and were created."
- Rev. 4:10-11

"Behold, I shew you a mystery; We shall not all sleep, but we shall all be changed, In a moment, in the twinkling of an eye, at the last trump: for the trumpet shall sound, and the dead shall be raised incorruptible, and we shall be changed." - I Cor. 15:51-52

"For the Lord himself shall descend from heaven with a shout, with the voice of the archangel, and with the trump of God: and the dead in Christ shall rise first: Then we which are alive and remain shall be caught up together with them in the clouds, to meet the Lord in the air: and so shall we ever be with the Lord."
- I Thess. 4:16-17.

Christ will return within visual range of the earth (the clouds, air), His angels shall gather up His servants to where He is, and return to Heaven. When Christ gathers His Bride (the Church), He will also gather the dead in Christ back to the time of His Ascension.
"...the dead in Christ shall rise first."

Christ's Gathering of His Ambassadors

Chronologically, right after Christ addresses the seven churches, He now calls John up to Heaven, picturing the gathering of the saints before the Tribulation period. The Church will be in Heaven during the Christ's wrath on the world and Satan's kingdom.

"Now then we are ambassadors for Christ, as though God did beseech you by us..." - II Cor. 5:20

Understanding The Tribulation Time

The time of the Tribulation is not a purgatory to purify the Christians (as some make it out to be) - **it it Christ's crushing the rebellion on Earth - breaking the will and kingdom of Satan.** Yes, there will be those who will be saved during this time, but before Christ starts the opening salvos and bombardments of Earth, He calls home His ambassadors - the Church.

World Defectors

*"Let no man deceive you by any means: for that day shall not come, except there come a **falling away** first, and that man of sin be revealed, the son of perdition..." - II Thess. 2:3*

Paul was a **Roman** (Acts 22:27), and was the **only apostle** who regularly used military terms and metaphors (fight, war, warfare, armour) that his audience and culture would be very familiar with in that day. The term **falling away** is a military term for physical desertion (Noah Websters 1828 Dictionary); **falling back** is the military term for strategic retreat.

Twice in Scripture prior, this terminology was used in this fashion (Jer. 38:19 and I Chron. 12:19). The term *falling away* is not found in Scripture referring to spiritual apostasy; although, even the term *apostasy* can mean physically leaving one's party (WD1828). Paul was telling the Thessalonians that the period of God's judgment will not come until Christ's faithful servants defect from this world and Satan, and are given (in a sense) assylum in Heaven. After that takes place, then the Antichrist will be revealed; and then that starts the time of judgment known as the Tribulation.

Jesus Christ specifically told His disciples that in the season He returns (Tribulation & judgment - the day of the Lord), it will be just like the days of Noah and Lot. In both of these patterns, Christ made sure His servants were called to safety before judgment came.

When Christ gathers His Bride (the Church), He will also gather the dead in Christ back to the time of His Ascension. *"...the dead in Christ shall rise first."*

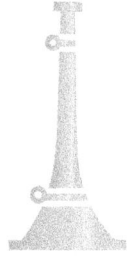

Suffering and Purification for Christians?

There is a false idea that Christians will not be raptured, and that they will go through the Tribulation period as a means of suffering and purification before Christ returns at the end; my friend, that is a false doctrine crept in from the hellish Catholic notion of purgatory and atoning for sins. The Scriptures are clear that there is nothing we can add to our salvation, and that when we stand before Him one day, accepted, it will be entirely because of what Christ has done for us, not because of what we endured or added to our salvation.

Over the centuries, most of the church has already died and gone into the presence of Christ - most of the church has already missed the Tribulation. We cannot add to our salvation, and Christ will never ask us to.

"...that evil servant shall say in his heart, My lord delayeth his coming..." - Matt. 24:48

Speaking to the church of Philadelphia: *"Because thou hast kept the word of my patience, I also will keep thee from the hour of temptation, which shall come upon all the world, to try them that dwell upon the earth."* - Rev. 3:10

*"And Abraham drew near, and said, Wilt thou also destroy the righteous with the wicked? Peradventure there be fifty righteous within the city: wilt thou also destroy and not spare the place for the fifty righteous that are therein? **That be far from thee to do after this manner, to slay the righteous with the wicked: and that the righteous should be as the wicked, that be far from thee: Shall not the Judge of all the earth do right?**"* - Gen. 18:23-25

The angels to Lot: *"Haste thee, escape thither; for I cannot do any thing till thou be come thither."* - Gen. 19:22

Scoffers Will Deny Christ's Return (II Peter 3:3-4)

This is not limited to only the unbelievers. Many Christians deny that Christ will deliver His faithful servants before wrath. The repeat exhortations to *Watch* are because you don't know when He is coming back. This warning can only apply before the Tribulation, since once it starts, the Bible gives the chronology of the rest. **When He returns at the end of the Tribulation, it won't be a surprise - even Satan and his armies will be waiting and watching for Him.**

One strong reason to believe that Satan will work false signs and wonders to seemingly excuse away the Rapture is because if he can do so, then he can seemingly dismiss the claims of the entire New Testament, especially Revelation regarding the Tribulation time period. He will make claims that the Bible is only full of fables and metaphors. He will then pull out all the stops to belittle God's Word and discredit what it claims - namely, that a man of Satan will come to deceive the world.

A contributing factor in the great deception will be that right after the Rapture there will probably be more so-called 'christians' left behind than true believers who are raptured. Many 'churches' and 'pastors' will be the largest chorus explaining the Rapture away, "because, look, we're still here..." Sadly, they will then also be deluded by Satan's lies. To be a Christian in name only, or membership only - yet not personally trust in Jesus Christ alone to save you, makes you no Christian at all.

*"...And when these things **begin to come to pass,** then look up, and lift up your heads; for your redemption draweth nigh. "*
- I Timothy 2:5

69

🐏 The Lamb

📖 *"...I saw in the right hand of him that sat on the throne a book written within and on the backside, sealed with seven seals. And I saw a strong angel proclaiming with a loud voice,* **Who is worthy to open the book, and to loose the seals thereof?**" - Rev. 5:1-2

"...behold, the **Lion** *of the tribe of Juda, the Root of David, hath prevailed to open the book, and to loose the seven seals thereof. And I beheld, and, lo, in the midst of the throne and of the four beasts, and in the midst of the elders, stood a* **Lamb** *as it had been slain ...And he came and took the book out of the right hand of him that sat upon the throne."*
- Rev. 5:5-6

Title Deed to Earth (Rev. 5, Jer. 32:6-15)
The Lamb, Jesus Christ, receives the title deed to earth - thus receiving the dominion, glory, and kingdom (Daniel 7:13-14). This is when Christ is given the scepter and right to rule over the earth. **The Tribulation time period is when Christ ascends to the throne, and puts down Satan's kingdom and rule.** He will use the Tribulation period to break them with a rod of iron (Psalm 2:9).

☁️ John In Heaven

Jesus Christ is called both a Lion and Lamb.

Lion: for His majesty and power; He is Judge and King.

Lamb: for His meekness; He is a Saviour, full of grace.

The Church Praises The Lamb

"...Thou art worthy to take the book, and to open the seals thereof:
for thou wast slain, and hast redeemed us to God by thy blood
out of every kindred, and tongue, and people, and nation;
and hast made us unto our God kings and priests:
and we shall reign on the earth."
- Rev. 5:5-9-10

*"...**Worthy is the Lamb that was slain to receive power**,*
and riches, and wisdom, and strength, and honour,
and glory, and blessing."
- Rev. 5:12

"...Blessing, and honour, and glory, and power,
be unto him that sitteth upon the throne,
and unto the Lamb for ever and ever."
- Rev. 5:13

The Tribulation time is when Christ takes back what is rightfully His.

The Seal Judgments

The 1st Seal - Antichrist

"...behold a white horse: and he that sat on him had a bow; and a crown was given unto him: and he went forth conquering, and to conquer. " - Rev. 6:5-6

Antichrist will arrive on the scene, appearing to bring peace initially, but he uses it to gain strategic advantage.

Notice that when he appears on the scene, he already has a measure of power and authority given to him.

Events Transpiring on Earth, John's perspective in Heaven.

The 2nd Seal - War

"...And there went out another horse that was red: and power was given to him that sat thereon to take peace from the earth, and that they should kill one another: and there was given unto him a great sword."
- Rev. 6:4

WWIII

The 3rd Seal - Famine

📖 *"...I beheld, and lo a black horse; and he that sat on him had a pair of balances in his hand. And I heard a voice in the midst of the four beasts say, A measure of wheat for a penny, and three measures of barley for a penny; and see thou hurt not the oil and the wine."* - Rev. 6:5-6

❗ As a result of World War III, food shortages, devastation to agricultural infrastructure and manpower, as well as economic collapse bring a swift domino effect of famine. The verse implies that it will take a day's wage to procure a loaf of bread - if any is available. The rich will be able to afford or procure goods, even luxury goods, with minor trouble.

❗ The 'perfect storm' of events leaves many in 'refugee status' with no/little access to food, water, medical supplies, protection, etc. - many will die as a direct result (Rev. 6:8).

❗ Those in the Tribulation: will probably see **at least** 50% of the people around them die horribly over next 7 years. The 'why' is because of God's wrath on the world (Isa. 26:21). Looking at the ongoing wars and disasters throughout this period, on top of the percentages stated by Scripture, it is not a stretch to conclude that less than a quarter of today's population will be remaining at the end of the Tribulation.

The 4th Seal - Death

"...behold a pale horse: and his name that sat on him was Death, and Hell followed with him. And power was given unto them over the fourth part of the earth, to kill with sword, and with hunger, and with death, and with the beasts of the earth." - Rev. 6:8

1/4th world's population decimated (Rev. 6:8) by the wars, resulting chaos, famine, and disease.

The 5th Seal - Persecution

"And when he had opened the fifth seal, I saw under the altar the souls of them that were slain for the word of God, and for the testimony which they held: and they cried with a loud voice, saying, How long, O Lord, holy and true, dost thou not judge and avenge our blood on them that dwell on the earth? And white robes were given unto every one of them; and it was said unto them, that they should rest yet for a little season, until their fellowservants also and their brethren, that should be killed as they were, should be fulfilled" - Rev. 6:9-11

Early on, those who turn to Christ will probably be blamed for the bulk of what is going on in the world. Persecution will come in various forms throughout this Tribulation period; in the latter half, beheading will be the common method (20:4).

The 6th Seal - Earthquake

Infrastructure

With the global great earthquake (on top of war damage), dams have burst, highways buckled, bridges wrecked, rails tangled, runways cracked, etc. This will not be quickly repaired, and will lead to vast shortages and deprivations in many areas. Many areas will simply not be rebuilt.

? Great tsunamis devastate coastal areas and islands.

? Modern communication access (internet, email, etc.) will most likely increasingly suffer blackouts and permanent outages, and taper off as critical regional infrastructure is damaged by the great earthquakes, loss of personnel, oceanic cables cut, etc. Toward the latter end, only limited satellite-based comms, military/government comm systems, ham radio, etc. may be functional. Limited internet comms may be reduced to dial-up systems. Even today we see governments building systems and bunkers to survive major calamities. These may be the only groups with reliable comm access toward the end. Rev. 16:5 implies many hide in bunkers after the sixth seal earthquake.

The 144,000

"And I saw another angel ascending from the east, having the seal of the living God: and he cried with a loud voice to the four angels, to whom it was given to hurt the earth and the sea, saying, Hurt not the earth, neither the sea, nor the trees, till we have sealed the servants of our God in their foreheads." - Rev. 7:2-3

Note that this sealing does not take place till after the first six trumpets; already over a quarter of earth's population has died.

144,000 Israelites Sealed (Rev. 7:4-8)

God has 12,000 Israelites selected from the various tribes of Israel as His messengers during the Tribulation time. The Church, the bride of Christ, is now in Heaven, and these witnesses (along with the two witnesses from God), proclaim the Gospel during this time. The opening events of the Tribulation have most likely opened their eyes and heart to see and accept their Messiah, and now tell the world about Him.

Rev. 14:4-5 tells us that these 144,000 are individuals who are single, and not necessarily tied up with spouse and children - thus they can travel and spread the Gospel more easily than others. In Matt. 24:19, Jesus remarked that it would be very hard on mothers during this time because of the war and disaster conditions. Sometimes God called people to celibacy because of austere conditions, as well as the culture in which they find themselves (Jer. 16:1-4). It also remarks that they have not defiled themselves with the rampant promiscuous fornication that will be prevalent in this time.

It appears that many of this number, along with the saved Gentiles, will be martyred during this period (Rev. 14:13). The only people stated as having divine protection during this time are the two witnesses, and only for a certain number of days.

John In Heaven

*"...I beheld, and, lo, a great multitude, which no man could number, of all nations, and kindreds, and people, and tongues, stood before the throne, and before the Lamb, clothed with white robes, and palms in their hands; and cried with a loud voice, saying, **Salvation to our God which sitteth upon the throne, and unto the Lamb.**"* - Rev. 7:9-10

His first entry in Jerusalem was on a donkey - He came as a Saviour and Lamb, signifying peace. When He returns to Earth and Jerusalem the next time, it will be on a horse - a true Triumphal Entry as King.

Palm branches signify victory

"And one of the elders answered, saying unto me, What are these which are arrayed in white robes? and whence came they? And I said unto him, Sir, thou knowest. And he said to me, These are they which came out of great tribulation, and have washed their robes, and made them white in the blood of the Lamb." - Rev. 7:13-14

Note that Scripture made a differentiation between the groups in heaven: the Church (already there, and represented by the elders) points out a separated group of saints who are still arriving (Tribulation martyrs, 6:11).

"...They shall hunger no more, neither thirst any more; neither shall the sun light on them, nor any heat. For the Lamb which is in the midst of the throne shall feed them, and shall lead them unto living fountains of waters: and God shall wipe away all tears from their eyes."
- Rev. 7:16-17

Trumpets 1-4

The 7th Seal - 7 Trumpets

Calm Before the Storm
At the opening of this seal, there is silence in Heaven for half an hour (Rev. 8:1) - the judgments that are coming after this are unlike anything which the world has ever seen.

"...I saw the seven angels which stood before God; and to them were given seven trumpets."
- Rev. 8:2

"...the smoke of the incense, which came with the prayers of the saints, ascended up before God out of the angel's hand. And the angel took the censer, and filled it with fire of the altar, and cast it into the earth..." - Rev. 8:4-5

The prayers of the all the saints are about to be answered...

Notice that the first four trumpet judgments *could* all be the result of Earth passing through the debris field from a large comet breakup.

Events Transpiring on Earth, John's perspective in Heaven.

1st Trumpet - Burning

"...there followed hail and fire mingled with blood, and they were cast upon the earth: and the third part of trees was burnt up, and all green grass was burnt up." - Rev. 8:7

2nd - Sea Smitten

"...and as it were a great mountain burning with fire was cast into the sea: and the third part of the sea became blood; and the third part of the creatures which were in the sea, and had life, died; and the third part of the ships were destroyed." - Rev. 8:8-9

This may be a large meteorite that strikes the sea, killing many fish with the compression waves (dynamite in lake effect), and forming massive rogue waves that swamp shipping.

3rd - Wormwood

"... there fell a great star from heaven, burning as it were a lamp, and it fell upon the third part of the rivers, and upon the fountains of waters; and the name of the star is called Wormwood: and the third part of the waters became wormwood; and many men died of the waters, because they were made bitter." - Rev. 8:10-11. Historically, some meteorites have been known to contain arsenic, and contaminate local well systems.

4th - Heavens Dimmed

"...the third part of the sun was smitten, and the third part of the moon, and the third part of the stars; so as the third part of them was darkened, and the day shone not for a third part of it, and the night likewise." - Rev. 8:12

"...I beheld, and heard an angel flying through the midst of heaven, saying with a loud voice, **Woe, woe, woe, to the inhabiters of the earth** by reason of the other voices of the trumpet of the three angels, which are yet to sound!" - Rev. 8:13

Trumpets 5-6

5th - Locusts

Satan Opens The Bottomless Pit (Rev. 9:1-4)

"...I saw a star fall from heaven unto the earth: and to him was given the key of the bottomless pit. And he opened the bottomless pit; and there arose a smoke out of the pit, as the smoke of a great furnace; and the sun and the air were darkened by reason of the smoke of the pit. And there came out of the smoke locusts upon the earth: and unto them was given power, as the scorpions of the earth have power. And it was commanded them that they should not hurt the grass of the earth, neither any green thing, neither any tree; but only those men which have not the seal of God in their foreheads."

Satan (the falling star, Isa. 12:12; Luke 10:18) is permitted to open the abyss and release some of the demons imprisoned there (II Pet. 2:4). Note that Scripture points out there is a literal gate to Hell, and that it will be opened, releasing enough smoke to dim the skies.

The locusts (which can fly) are given the ability to sting like scorpions (v.3). They will most likely continue to fly in swarms, attacking any who do not have the mark of God in the foreheads. This will continue for five months.

*"And to them it was given that they should not kill them, but that they should be tormented five months: and their torment was as the torment of a scorpion, when he striketh a man. And in those days **shall men seek death, and shall not find it;** and shall desire to die, and death shall flee from them."* - Rev. 9:5-6

Notice that Satan has already used **his media** to prepare and condition the world to normalize the concept of a zombie.

Events Transpiring on Earth, John's perspective in Heaven.

83

"And they had a king over them, which is the angel of the bottomless pit, whose name in the Hebrew tongue is Abaddon, but in the Greek tongue hath his name Apollyon." - Rev. 9:11

These creatures are either demons themselves, or creatures possessed and controlled by them.

"One woe is past; and, behold, there come two woes more hereafter." - Rev. 9:12

6th - Fallen Angels

Fallen Angels Released (Rev. 9:14-15)
*"...Loose the four angels which are bound in the great river Euphrates. And the four angels were loosed, which were prepared for an hour, and a day, and a month, and a year, for **to slay the third part of men.** And the number of the army of the horsemen were two hundred thousand thousand: and I heard the number of them."*

These fallen angels are so evil that they, apparently, have been bound since their initial fall. The Euphrates is very significant: the Garden of Eden was in this area (Gen. 2:14), the fall of man, the tower of Babel, as well as Babylon and its many pagan gods.

There has been speculation that this large army (200,000,000) is China, as they are the only ones currently who can field such an army. I tend to think that this is a demonic army, since they are commanded by these four fallen angels, and apparently come out of the pit as well.

1/3 of the remaining mankind killed, on top of the previous 1/4.

Currently (2013), the world has an estimated 7.127 billion people. If we generously assume 127 million people (1.78%) are gathered to Christ before the Tribulation, that leaves 7 billion.

1/4 = 1,750,000,000 dead; 5,250,000,000 remain.

1/3 = 1,750,000,000 additional dead; 3,500,000,000 remain.

50% of the world's population is dead in the first 3.5 yrs of the Tribulation.

200,000,000 Chinese?

China's current population 1,350,000,000 people. If they suffer an average 50% loss of their population, they are down to 675,000,000. With such a toll on their country, and the need for trained personnel just to maintain order with the scope of disasters, I highly doubt even they would be in a position to field and sustain an army of 200,000,000 - which would be almost a third of their remaining population. Also note that the number refers to the horsemen - that wouldn't include the large number of logistical supply forces needed to sustain such an army. I believe the army referred to is demonic in origin, and not human. This may be Satan's army that later battles the angels in Heaven before Satan and his army is cast out (Rev. 12:9).

"And the rest of the men which were not killed by these plagues yet repented not of the works of their hands, ***that they should not worship devils, and idols*** *of gold, and silver, and brass, and stone, and of wood: which neither can see, nor hear, nor walk: neither repented they of their murders,* ***nor of their sorceries,*** *nor of their fornication, nor of their thefts."* - Rev. 9:20-21

The Seven Thunders

Earth Claimed For Christ (Rev. 10:1-2)

"...I saw another mighty angel come down from heaven, clothed with a cloud: and a rainbow was upon his head, and his face was as it were the sun, and his feet as pillars of fire: And he had in his hand a little book open: and he set his right foot upon the sea, and his left foot on the earth..."

Seven Thunders (Rev. 10:3-4)

"And cried with a loud voice, as when a lion roareth: and when he had cried, seven thunders uttered their voices. And when the seven thunders had uttered their voices, I was about to write: and I heard a voice from heaven saying unto me, Seal up those things which the seven thunders uttered, and write them not."

Mystery of God Is To Be Finished (Rev. 10:7)

"...in the days of the voice of the seventh angel, when he shall begin to sound, the mystery of God should be finished, as he hath declared to his servants the prophets."

God's working throughout history and prophecy will now be brought to a completion in this final portion of days of the seventh trumpet. There may be a lot of our understanding (in Heaven and on Earth) finally opened in this time period as we see God's hand, down through time, finally completing His marvelous work.

John is told to eat the little book that the angel was holding, and that it was sweet to taste, but bitter to the belly (v.10). God's revelation of what is about to unfold upon the world is bittersweet and somber - Christ will set up His kingdom and fulfill His Word and prophecy - but there will be much judgment before all things are completed.

John In Heaven

The 7th Trumpet

Revelation chapter 11 covers an overview of the two witnesses; When they finish, there is an earthquake in Jerusalem (11:13). Also, the 7th Trumpet is sounded, signaling the start of the seven bowl judgments (11:15).

The Two Witnesses prophesy for 1,260 days - the first half of the Tribulation.

Earthquake in Jerusalem kills 7,000 (Rev. 11:13).

Last Trump?

Do not confuse the last trump of I Cor. 15 with the seventh trumpet of Revelation (11:15); contextually, I Cor. 15:51-52 is God's voice - sounding as a trumpet (compare Rev. 1:10), whilst the seventh trumpet is a literal trumpet (Rev. 8:2). Paul (in I Cor.) is referring to the calling of the Lord to His children to come up hither. The Revelation seventh trumpet is a trumpet blast of approaching judgment.

"*And the seventh angel sounded; and there were great voices in heaven, saying,* **The kingdoms of this world are become the kingdoms of our Lord, and of his Christ; and he shall reign for ever and ever.** *And the four and twenty elders, which sat before God on their seats, fell upon their faces, and worshipped God, saying, We give thee thanks, O Lord God Almighty, which art, and wast, and art to come; because* **thou hast taken to thee thy great power, and hast reigned.**" - Rev. 11:15-17

Events Transpiring on Earth, John's perspective in Heaven.

The Two Witnesses

Since Christ has called and gathered up His bride, the church, to Heaven, these two witnesses will be on earth, spreading the Gospel, in the first half of the Tribulation (Rev. 11:3). Two witnesses are needed to establish the certainty of any truth (Deut. 17:6).

The fact that God has to send two witnesses during the first half of the Tribulation says a lot about what happened to the church - they are gone. In the now spiritually dark world, God sends "two candlesticks" (Rev. 11:4) since His seven candlesticks (the church as a whole, Rev. 1:20) is gone.

While we know that one is Elijah (Mal. 4:5), it is speculation to guess who the other is. Some have suggested that he may be John the Baptist, since John referred to himself as the friend of the bridegroom (John 3:29). These two witnesses can do the same wonders as Elijah - call down fire and call for drought, as well as of Moses, turning water into blood (Rev. 11:6).

After 3.5 years (1,260 days) of giving their testimony to what God is doing, the Antichrist kills them in Jerusalem (Rev. 11:7). The world's hatred for them is so great that they leave their bodies in the street to rot (11:9). After 3.5 days, they come back to life (v.11). God calls them to Him in the same manner as He did His Church...

"Come up hither. And they ascended up to heaven in a cloud; and their enemies beheld them." - Rev. 11:12

Note that Scripture does not say the entire world watches (live) the two witnesses die or come back to life; but that *"they of"* (also implies a portion) the world's population hear about it and send gifts; a much smaller portion actually sees them rise from the dead (Rev. 11:1). We can infer that over the course of the three and a half days since their murder that news was communicated around the world to those that could receive it. Again, sustained infrastructure damage, but the Antichrist will at least have some systems of communication and propaganda.

Events Transpiring on Earth, John's perspective in Heaven.

The Antichrist

The Bible records that before Noah's Flood, fallen angels had procreated with some of mankind (Gen. 6:2-5; Jude 1:6). According to Matthew 24:37, the end times will be like the days of Noah. It shouldn't surprise us then that Satan would be involved in creating an offspring specifically for deceiving the world, especially one to embody himself.

Many of the ancient false gods were based on pre-Flood deities (based on fallen angel offspring) which were depicted as half-man and half-creature, possessing human and non-human traits and abilities.

Antichrist, son of Satan, Gen 3:15

He will be extremely intelligent (Daniel 7:8, 8:23), and will initially appear to be the saviour of the world. It will probably be very unpopular to call him the Antichrist.

Revelation refers to the Antichrist as "...*the beast...*" - Rev 13

He will probably not be entirely portrayed as alien - only partially. He will probably have many humanoid characteristics, with human DNA - and Satan's DNA (seed of the serpent - Gen. 3:15). It would be Satan's counterfeit and imitation of the incarnation of Jesus Christ, the son of God; except Satan will be making the son the Satan. Mimicking Christ's genealogical right, the Antichrist will possibly be of, or associated with, the occult-backed Merovingian (Dragon) Dynasty (Rev. 12:9). Daniel 11:37 implies Antichrist may be either a sodomite or androgynous (both genders).

Antichrist will genetically be an European Israelite, possibly of the tribe of Dan - Daniel 11:37. Human-wise, as an 11th king, he will rise out of a group of 10 nations (Dan. 7:8, Rev. 17:17).

His arrival/revealing will be unparalleled

"...whose [Antichrist's] coming is after the working of Satan with all power and signs and lying wonders, and with all deceivableness of unrighteousness **...strong delusion, that they should believe a lie...**" - II Thessalonians 2:9-11

"...that he might be revealed in his time." - II Thessalonians 2:6
The Antichrist will not rise up through the normally expected political ranks - he will be revealed and then given power.

He will reassert the original lie

In the Garden of Eden, Satan took on a form of a beautiful serpent (avatar) to deceive Eve (Gen. 3:1). *"And the serpent said ...ye shall be as gods, knowing good and evil."* - Genesis 3:4-5

He will make craft (the occult) to prosper (Daniel 8:25). Knowledge of esoteric material and symbols will be heavily promoted and widely practiced. This will include much of the pre-Flood occult worship, pagan rituals, and debauchery. **The Bible tells us that these are expressly forbidden (Deut. 18:10-12).** He will probably revive pagan use of sacred sites around the world for their original purposes - contacting the forbidden spirit world, and claiming that humans can ascend to god-like planes of existence - all if they fall down and worship him.

Antichrist's Character
"And the beast which I saw was like unto a leopard, and his feet were as the feet of a bear, and his mouth as the mouth of a lion: and the dragon gave him his power, and his seat, and great authority." - Rev. 13:2

Leopard - represents the Graeco-Macedonian Empire, culture and influence (Dan 7:6).

Bear's Feet - represents the Media-Persian Empire (Dan 7:5) and pagan splendor and wealth.

Lion's Mouth - represents Babylonian autocracy and power (Dan. 7:4).

Deadly Wound

Since the way the beast is described in context and previous prophecies (Daniel), it appears that this deadly wound is nor referring to a literal medical condition, per se, but rather the apparent demise of the said governments, namely the Roman Empire. Technically, the Roman Empire did not die, it just fell apart, but today it has been revived largely through the European Union. When the Antichrist comes on the scene, this former Roman Empire will be fully restored. With that, though, the verse is also applied to a man, so it can be expected that the Antichrist will fake a resurrection in an attempt to counterfeit the power of Christ.

> A great many of the saints are more interested in Antichrist than they are in Christ.
>
> *- Dr. Gaebelein*

Problem / Solution

Global economic depression and failure, middle east regional chaos, scandals, turmoil, etc. are managed symptoms to create a world where people long for a strong leader who can act decisively and powerfully - and they will gladly give up freedom and national notions to one whom they think can bypass all the legislative gridlock and just get done what needs to be done. In other words, the world will now globally have the ripeness that pre-Hitler Germany experienced that made it so easy for Hitler to ascend to power. It also creates a strong willingness to ignore or allow power and moral abuses. It is a fostered longing for a strong leader that makes many overlook certain aspects, and actually endears even a critic - all because they want to be part of his movement and what he is accomplishing.

"These have one mind, and shall give their power and strength unto the beast."
- Rev. 17:13

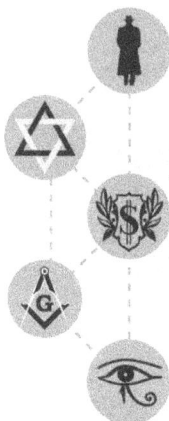

Antichrist, son of Satan,
Gen 3:15

The Antichrist is one who has been specifically born and bred, groomed, and satanically prepared for his role.

"For God hath put in their hearts to fulfil his will, and to agree, and give their kingdom unto the beast, until the words of God shall be fulfilled."
- Rev. 17:17

"And he shall confirm the covenant with many for one week..." - *Daniel 9:27*

Peace/truce treaty is brokered, with many signatories, most likely the remaining former immediate neighbors of Israel.

Tribulation Deceptions*

> **!** There is a *LOT* of misinformation out about some of these perspectives and points - this section is only food for thought, since the Bible deliberately does not say what the delusion will be.

*"...whose [Antichrist's] coming is after the working of Satan with all power and signs and lying wonders, and with all deceivableness of unrighteousness ...**strong delusion, that they should believe a lie...**"* - II Thessalonians 2:9-11

Satan is known as:
"...the prince of the power of the air..." - Ephesians 2:2

Some have speculated that the increasing UFO sightings and abductions are both by Satan and his angels for a program of acclimatization and a mask of their repeat of procreation with humans (Genesis 6) - which Jesus Christ warned would mark the end days (Matt. 24:37). The Book of Jasher, an extra-biblical script yet referenced in the Bible (Joshua 10:13, II Sam. 1:18), also mentions the mixing of species in provoking the Lord that occurred (Jasher 4:18).

"... their horsemen shall come from far; they shall fly as the eagle that hasteth to eat." - Hab. 1:8
The simile of the eagle implies very fast movement, often straight down, as when an eagle attacks its prey.

"...the magnitude of a lie always contains a certain factor of credibility since the great masses of people ...more easily fall victim to a big lie than to a little one."
- Adolf Hitler

93

Portraying themselves as benevolent aliens, Satan's fallen angels (or their offspring), deceive the world with their humanoid characteristics and abilities, and their enviable technology and power (Dan 8:24). As part of the delusion, they may claim that they removed the believers who were raptured. They may claim that those who disappeared were not ready for their New Age cosmic shift, and are actually left behind in a former dimension.

The sudden appearance of multiple UFOs would largely halt various conflicts, and post-rapture chaos, and quickly get the major nations to start working together (with the populace's support), with sovereignty matters no longer a top concern. These deceivers may utilize suppressed technology to dismantle earth's nuclear programs, and other acts to win mankind's affection and trust.

To further convince mankind that they are all powerful, and are the one's behind 'the disappearances', Satan and his followers may fake aspects of the rapture, with the queen of heaven reassuring the world that they shouldn't worry, and that the world will be going through some more earth changes as part of reaching some higher level. This deception would possibly involve using satellites to broadcast video messages onto the ionosphere, similar to older televisions and crts; audio means can be accomplished in similar manner (Project Blue Beam).

If Damascus is destroyed with a nuclear weapon, then the Antichrist might be revealed under the pretense of extraterrestrials intervening in mankind's 'path to destruction'. He would then be seen as a mediator capable of brokering a covenant with Israel - and also one who had the appearance of power capable of enforcing the treaty.

Hegelian Dialect & Cognitive Dissonance?

Thesis: Use mass media to condition four generations that aliens are threatening, advanced, powerful, and predatory.

Anti-thesis: Have aliens revealed that are the polar opposite - long involved in earth history, intelligent, and come to solve major world problems.

Synthesis: Beings that are perceived as intelligent, spiritual, advanced caretakers - but expected to rule with an iron rod, crushing any resistance.

What the general populace is not told (and will not believe) is that the G20 nations have known about the technology and fallen angels for many decades, and have worked clandestinely in preparing the way for Satan. For decades, military leadership has known the source of these unexplained event - internal programs of our nation, or others. In the right time, they will have disclosure to the public that they knew, and have worked with the media to acclimate and normalize the public to their existence, and avoid chaos.

It is well known that the Nazis were in development of flying saucers (Rundflugzeug, Feuerball, Diskus, Haunebu, V7, etc.), although specifics are scant. Considering the level of occult k nowledge that they sought (Armanen) and received, along with historical insights, it is thought that this project was much more developed than initially led to believe after the war. This technology, and others, was apparently what was secreted out of German in the final stages of war. Considering that this was over 65 years ago, this technology was most likely honed and finalized decades ago.

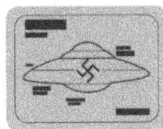

It would not be a stretch to suspect that the luciferian-minded scientists involved in the US Operation Paperclip eventually also collaborated on further development of this technology. While speculation may continue, for us it is enough to highly suspect that this technology (and those behind it) will play a vital role in Antichrist's massive deception. **The Nazi regime is dead and gone - our main concern today is who their research and technology was handed over to, and for what causes.**

Food for thought: on average, the military complex has access to secret weapons and technology that is 10 years more advanced than civilians. On top of that, there are also suppressed advanced technologies known and controlled by very tight circles, for varying reasons.

Some of these may have been obtained from pre-Flood occult relics or related knowledge revealed by demonic channeling (expressly forbidden by God - Deut. 18:9-12). Satan, and his human friends, will be using many of these in their demonstration of hitherto unseen power.

Without an universal belief in the new age religion and doctrines, the success of the Antichrist's new global order will be impossible. To that end, the dominant monotheistic groups (Islam, Catholic, Christian) will have to be nullified or greatly reduced. The first 3.5 years will be using his deceptions and tricks to convince the world religions that they have a common core faith. Again, you cannot have a unified world with fractured faiths; but it will take some time to tear down all walls of resistance. Some will collapse quicker than others, depending on whether their personal faith was just a form of religion. Stage 1 will probably be false signs and wonders to back up the assertions of 'the gods visiting', and perhaps a slick, false demonstration/explanation of the Rapture. Stage 2 will probably present false evidence/signs that discredit, or causes, a breakdown, or re-evaluation, of archeological knowledge. These 'discoveries' will point and draw people to the concept of a greater, shared faith core, and require 'corrections' about major religious tenets and doctrines - and affirm Stage 1 claims.

*"Now the Spirit speaketh expressly, that in the latter times some shall depart from the faith, giving heed to **seducing spirits,** and **doctrines of devils**..."* - I Timothy 4:1

The world has already seen how easily it can be deceived with just a handful of forged primary artifacts, ignorance of solid contradictory evidence, mountains of unproven theories, and fantasy conjecture. Part of its success is that the human heart wants evolution to be true so they are not accountable to some higher being for their actions. When we look at how much the spiritual state of our world has shifted just within this one generation lifespan, we shouldn't be surprised to see that we are now ripe with people who will readily latch onto any deception that justifies their rejection of God.

Tribulation Midpoint

Chapter 12 is both the midpoint of the Tribulation and the book (11/11). This chapter sees the Antichrist/Satan turn against Israel.

*"And there was war in heaven: Michael and his angels fought against the dragon; and the dragon fought and his angels, And prevailed not; neither was their place found any more in heaven. And the great dragon was cast out, that old serpent, called the Devil, and Satan, which deceiveth the whole world: **he was cast out into the earth, and his angels were cast out with him.**"* - Revelation 12:7-9

Apparently, this midpoint is when Satan's proverbial wings are clipped, and he's confined to Earth. This *might* also imply *some* of his technological wonder works might not be available or useable any more.

*"Woe to the inhabiters of the earth and of the sea! for the devil is come down unto you, having great wrath, because **he knoweth that he hath but a short time.** And when the dragon saw that **he was cast unto the earth,** he persecuted the woman [the nation Israel] which brought forth the man child."* - Revelation 12:12-13

Jewish Persecution
With the Antichrist now in control of the Temple Mount, and Jerusalem, he starts a campaign to destroys the Jews. The Bible warns them that when they see the Temple defiled by him, that they are to immediately **flee** to the mountains - where God will sustain and protect them supernaturally (Rev. 12:6,14-16).

🌐 **Events Transpiring on Earth,** John's perspective in Heaven.

Abomination of Desolation

Satan knows he will never be able to ascend onto the throne of God in Heaven; so he does the closest thing to it - the earthly seat of God - the holy place in the Temple. This is why he, and his occult followers, desire the Temple to be rebuilt; so he can go before the Ark which contains the commandments of God, and break them at the very symbolic earthly throne of God.

"...he shall exalt himself, and magnify himself above every god, and shall speak marvellous things against the God of gods..." - Daniel 11:36

"Who opposeth and exalteth himself above all that is called God, or that is worshipped; so that he as God sitteth in the temple of God, shewing himself that he is God." - Daniel 11:36

"...and in the midst of the week he shall cause the sacrifice and the oblation to cease, and for the overspreading of abominations..." - Daniel 9:27

- -

*"When ye therefore shall see the abomination of desolation, spoken of by Daniel the prophet, stand in the holy place, (whoso readeth, let him understand:) Then let them which be in Judaea **flee** into the mountains."*
- Matthew 24:15

When this event takes place, do not hesitate - flee immediately from the area of Jerusalem to the mountains. EVACUATE.

Further Reading: Matthew 24:15-22, Revelation 12:6

📖 Woman & Dragon Celestial Sign

*"And there appeared a great **wonder** in heaven; a woman **clothed with the sun,** and the **moon under her feet,** and upon her head **a crown of twelve stars:** And she **being with child** cried, travailing in birth, and pained to be delivered. And there appeared **another wonder** in heaven; and behold a great **red dragon,** having **seven heads** and **ten horns,** and **seven crowns upon his heads."***
- Revelation 12:1-3

The Greek word for *wonder* (G4592) here can also be translated **sign**.
"...there appeared a great sign in heaven..."

ASTRONOMY LESSON:

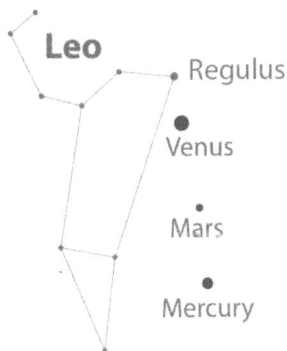

Leo

Regulus

Venus

Mars

Mercury

Sun

Virgo

Jupiter

● Moon

"moon under her feet"

Leo normally has 9 stars; however, on this date, it will have three planets in alignment as well, forming *"a crown of twelve stars..."*

Virgo will be obscured - *"clothed by the sun."* This arrangement will be during the day, as viewed from Jerusalem, Israel.

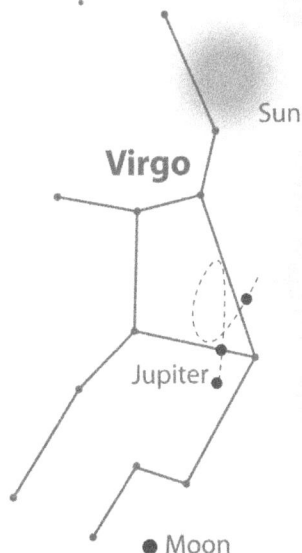

On 11/20/16, Jupiter (the king planet) enters the constellation Virgo (conception).

Jupiter enters retrograde motion, and is within the constellation for 41 weeks (normal pregnancy) till 9/9/17.

On 9/23/13, Jupiter will be passing through her legs - *"being with child."*

✳ *This celestial arrangement (verified with Stellarium software), is displayed looking straight up in the sky. Looking at the horizon, toward Virgo, it all would be rotated, with Virgo lying on her back, with the moon even more so "under her feet."*

This astronomical lineup will only occur on **Sept. 23, 2017,** and will not happen again till much further in the distant future.

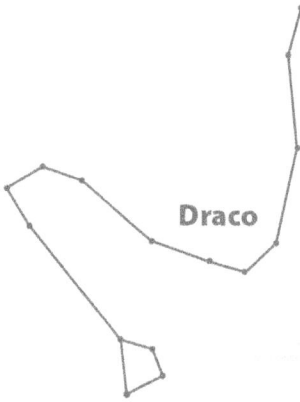

Draco used to be called the Great Dragon, as one of its stars, Thuban, used to be the pole star around 3000 BC.

Draco

Draco's head does have seven stars (**seven heads**) though commonly displayed as only four stars on most charts. (Gamma Draconis - companion red dwarf star, Nu Draconis - binary v1 & v2 Draconis, Beta Draconis - Binary with dwarf star companion)

The constellation Draconis (The Dragon, or Serpent) is also called the **red dragon** because one of its stars (R Draconis) is a red Mira-type variable star - a pulsating variable star characterized by very red colors. It is a red giant star. The dragon is being described as **red**, which is not mentioned again - anywhere in scripture. These specific descriptions in these verses also show that this is a literal, physical celestial scene that sparks the discussion and symbolic references in the rest of the chapter.

Bootes generally means *herdsman*, but gets it name from the Latin bovis, *"cow"*. Also called Great Horn in Chinese astronomy. **Ten horns.**

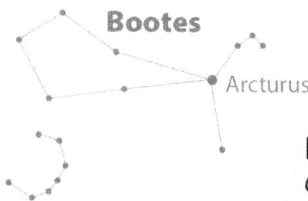

Bootes

Arcturus

Corona Borealis

Latin name literally means *'northern crown'*, and is made up of 7 stars. The 7 crowns above Draco's **seven heads**.

Sept. 23, 2017 + 1,260 days = **Mar. 6, 2021**

One reason we know this is more than a symbolic event is that God tells us how many days are remaining in the Tribulation after this sign - 1,260 days (Rev. 12:6).

👥 The Beasts

Rev 13 covers details on the Antichrist, False Prophet, Mark of the Beast implementation, and worship of the image.

Antichrist Blasphemes both God and His Bride, the Church

"And he opened his mouth in blasphemy against God, to blaspheme his name, and his tabernacle, and them that dwell in heaven." - Rev. 13:6

The False Prophet (Rev. 13:11).

Is also referred to as a beast. Has ability to do great wonders, such as calling fire down from heaven (Rev. 13:13-14); however, Scripture clarifies that he can do these wonders deceitfully by 'means' - e.g. they're hi-tech fakes. He may assume the esoteric title of Brother Truth - the right hand man who interprets the pagan religious law as prescribed by the Antichrist.

The Tribulation Saints Sorely Persecuted

"And it was given unto him to make war with the saints, and to overcome them: and power was given him over all kindreds, and tongues, and nations." - Rev. 13:7

Christ's Promises That Antichrist Will Be Overcome

"If any man have an ear, let him hear. He that leadeth into captivity shall go into captivity: he that killeth with the sword must be killed with the sword. Here is the patience and the faith of the saints." - Rev. 13:9-10

🌐 **Events Transpiring on Earth,** John's perspective in Heaven.

The Mark of the Beast Implemented (Rev. 14:9)

As a sign of allegiance and fidelity to the Antichrist's deity (e.g. that he is God) will be to receive his mark. It will most likely be a form of the star of Molech (Amos 5:26, Acts 7:43), often mistakenly labeled as the star of David. This is Satan's counterfeit to Jesus Christ, the Star of Jacob (Num. 24:17). Likely given in an occult 'marriage' rite equivalent to the wedding band - married to the Beast. This badge also gives one the 'right' to conduct transactions. 'Idolaters' (true Christians who refuse to worship the Beast as God) will be hated and beheaded (Daniel 7:25). **There will be no confusion about what the Mark represents - total rejection of the true God.**

Although mentioned more in-depth in chapter 14, the Antichrist *might* start implementing the mark of the beast at this Tribulation turning point.

"...If any man worship the beast and his image, and receive his mark in his forehead, or in his hand, the same shall drink of the wine of the wrath of God, which is poured out without mixture into the cup of his indignation; and he shall be tormented with fire and brimstone in the presence of the holy angels, and in the presence of the Lamb: and the smoke of their torment ascendeth up for ever and ever: and they have no rest day nor night, who worship the beast and his image, and whosoever receiveth the mark of his name." - Revelation 14:9-11*

Historical Precedent: Jews were denied service and business. Even Germans were denied service in many restaurants if they didn't do the Nazi salute. It is a mark of allegiance.

"...and I saw the souls of them that were beheaded for the witness of Jesus, and for the word of God, and which had not worshipped the beast, neither his image, neither had received his mark upon their foreheads, or in their hands; and they lived and reigned with Christ a thousand years." - Daniel 11:32-35

"...if thou shalt confess with thy mouth the Lord Jesus, and shalt believe in thine heart that God hath raised him from the dead, thou shalt be saved." - I Timothy 2:5

Visual Identification

Throughout Scripture, whenever someone was marked, it was always for visual identification. The Mark of the Beast, likewise, will be a visual indicator (not a microchip) that can instantly identify which side you are on. This badge of allegiance will not be dependant on any technology, and its use will extend beyond solely commerce. Your hand and your forehead are the two areas of your body most noticeable in any situation, and usually not obstructed from view.

"...the LORD set a mark upon Cain,
lest any finding him should kill him." - Gen. 4:15

"...And he called to the man clothed with linen, which had the writer's inkhorn by his side; and the LORD said unto him, Go through the midst of the city, through the midst of Jerusalem, and set a mark upon the foreheads of the men that sigh and that cry for all the abominations that be done in the midst thereof. " - Eze 9:3-4

Satan may roll out a microchip-based control measure in the first half of the Tribulation, but judging from the amount of infrastructure damage during that time, I don't think it will be effective. Not till the second half does he apparently link his new mark of allegiance - obtained in a luciferic initiation.

The Image of the Beast (Rev. 13:15)

"...he had power to give life unto the image of the beast, that the image of the beast should both speak, and cause that as many as would not worship the image of the beast should be killed." - Rev. 13:15

There is speculation on what this image of the beast will be, but there is reason to think that it might be an artificial intelligence that supposedly becomes aware, and interacts with humans. Such a device would, in a sense, be the pinnacle of human achievement - creating 'life' without God.

Mankind is made in the image of God; the beast will make something in symbolical image of man(kind). Tied into the global network, it could essentially be a global entity.

In the end, however, it will not be truly alive; only God can give true life, and later at the end of the Tribulation, when the antichrist and false prophet are thrown into the lake of fire, the image of the beast is not mentioned. It is simply destroyed or shut down, whatever it is.

Notice that the verse specifies that it is the image, itself, that cause non-worshippers to be put to death; in other words, it is aware, and it has the ability to give the command to put someone to death.

One of the greatest insults to our Creator is to have His own creation reject Him, and worship their own creation instead (Rom. 1:25).

Although mentioned more in-depth in chapter 13, the Antichrist *might* use this image or fabrication as part of the desolation set up in the Temple.

Queen of Heaven's Final Act?

Revelation 12 strongly indicates that the midpoint when Satan makes this move is Sept. 23, 2017, based on the celestial arrangement described there of the woman constellation with a crown of 12 stars above her head. Satan, and his followers, *appears likely* to paint and portray this event as the pagan queen of heaven, Ishtar, giving birth and way to Satan to be worshipped as the king of heaven. At this point, Satan and his image demands to be worshipped alone as *"the God of gods."*

"...Thou shalt worship the Lord thy God, and him only shalt thou serve." - Lk 4:8

Interlude

Revelation 14 is a pause where further explanation and orientation of the surrounding events takes place. It also gives an heavenly perspective of what upcoming events are, in the big picture. It is looking forward toward the end.

---

*"And I saw another angel fly in the midst of heaven, having the everlasting gospel to preach unto them that dwell on the earth, and to every nation, and kindred, and tongue, and people, saying with a loud voice, **Fear God, and give glory to him; for the hour of his judgment is come:** and worship him that made **heaven**, and **earth**, and the **sea**, and the **fountains of waters**."* - Rev. 14:6-7

By now, Satan has defiled the Temple, and set himself and his image up for worship, as well as implemented his mark. God sends one final messenger to unmistakably give the final broadcasted call to worship God, and follow Him only. He openly declares that God is the Creator who made everything. This is also the final warning - that the start of the fiercest judgments from God is now come.

"Here is the patience of the saints: here are they that keep the commandments of God, and the faith of Jesus. And I heard a voice from heaven saying unto me, Write, Blessed are the dead which die in the Lord from henceforth: Yea, saith the Spirit, that they may rest from their labours; and their works do follow them." - Rev. 14:12-13

Even though the world is going through tribulation and judgment, and the tribulation saints are enduring persecution, they can patiently endure because of God's promised reward for their faithfulness.

"And I looked, and behold a white cloud, and upon the cloud one sat like unto the Son of man, having on his head a golden crown, and in his hand a sharp sickle. And another angel came out of the temple, crying with a loud voice to him that sat on the cloud, Thrust in thy sickle, and reap: for the time is come for thee to reap; for the harvest of the earth is ripe." - Rev. 14:14-15. A symbolic, heavenly perspective and overview of what is about to transpire.

Tribulation Second Half

Ezekiel 38-39 describes how a confederacy (made of different nations than the first confederacy) move to attack Israel. The prophecy mentions that at this time Israel is in the midst of the (promised) land (a much larger portion than the present day state), that they dwell safely (not closely surrounded by all hostile nation states), and that they have acquired incredible wealth. When Russia and her allies move to attack, other nations ask if the move is to plunder and spoil this new resource-rich nation.

It appears that this may take place shortly after the mid-point of the Tribulation. The reason Russia needs allies is because Israel now has much more armament and resources to sustain much larger battles. Many of these surrounding nations have been negatively affected by the incredible regional power shift.

The confederacy will be destroyed by God Himself (Ezekiel 38-39) through fire, hailstones, pestilence, etc. It will take seven months to bury the dead (39:12).

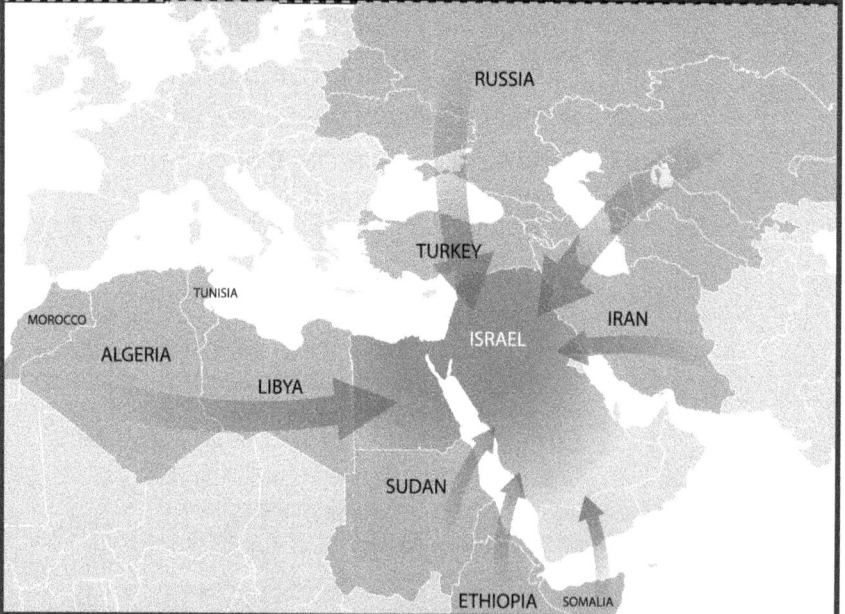

"Pray for the peace of Jerusalem: they shall prosper that love thee. Peace be within thy walls, and prosperity within thy palaces. For my brethren and companions' sakes, I will now say, Peace be within thee." - Psalm 122:6-8

God has a special plan for His chosen people, the Hebrews. As Christians, our deeds and actions can be a determining difference in many of their lives and decisions for Jesus Christ. We should use discernment and discretion in all that we do, but above all having love and charity. This book is prepared to aid your discernment on the proper focus and direction of our affection toward His people, and events pertaining to the land of Israel and Jerusalem.

Whose Side Are You On?

Many Christians do not consider that Satan and his various orders study prophetic events very closely, and know how to craft agendas to further their goals of influence by directly recruiting church support for 'religious' causes that seem to promote agendas of prophetic importance. Christians should be wise in all matters, not pawns. Because of its ultimate agenda goal to blaspheme God:

• Christians should not endorse or support the Temple rebuilding efforts in any way whatsoever - would be aiding and abetting the enemy.

• Christians should disassociate from any promotion or use of the pagan star of Molech.

• We should support noble causes that help the people of God (the Hebrews) - but not the people of Satan.

• Shun organizations that promote inter-faith, experiences, mysticism, and blurring of doctrine.

👑 Just and True

"...I saw another sign in heaven, great and marvellous, seven angels having the seven last plagues; for in them is filled up the wrath of God." - Rev. 15:1

Christ-Focused

Revelation is not about the Antichrist, Armageddon, four horsemen of the apocalypse, or other titillating events - it is solely centered around Jesus Christ. Woven throughout the book are the hosts of heaven praising Christ for what He is doing in claiming His kingdom, and judging wickedness. When studying Revelation, keep your focus where it should be, and you will see the true picture and reason for Revelation.

"And I saw as it were a sea of glass mingled with fire: and them that had gotten the victory over the beast, and over his image, and over his mark, and over the number of his name, stand on the sea of glass, having the harps of God. And they sing the song of Moses the servant of God, and the song of the Lamb, saying, Great and marvellous are thy works, Lord God Almighty; just and true are thy ways, thou King of saints. Who shall not fear thee, O Lord, and glorify thy name? for thou only art holy: for all nations shall come and worship before thee; for thy judgments are made manifest." - Rev. 15:2-4

🌥 John In Heaven

The Seven Bowls

The last seven plagues bring upon Earth judgments of the scale that the world has never seen before. It also marks the start of the gathering in Armageddon. It will take some time for them to gather, and then to make their way down toward Jerusalem. The word used as *"vial"* in the text was a broad shallow cup, not too unlike a bowl.

Boils on Antichrist's followers

"...there fell a noisome and grievous sore upon the men which had the mark of the beast, and upon them which worshipped his image." - Rev. 16:2

Sea becomes blood

"...poured out his vial upon the sea; and it became as the blood of a dead man: and every living soul died in the sea." - Rev. 16:3

Events Transpiring on Earth, John's perspective in Heaven.

Rivers and springs become blood

"...poured out his vial upon the rivers and fountains of waters; and they became blood." - Rev. 16:4

"...heard the angel of the waters say, Thou art righteous, O Lord, which art, and wast, and shalt be, because thou hast judged thus. For they have shed the blood of saints and prophets, and thou hast given them blood to drink; for they are worthy." - Rev. 16:5-6

"...I heard another out of the altar say, Even so, Lord God Almighty, true and righteous are thy judgments." - Rev. 16:5-6

Sun scorches mankind

"...poured out his vial upon the sun; and power was given unto him to scorch men with fire. And men were scorched with great heat, and blasphemed the name of God, which hath power over these plagues: and they repented not to give him glory." - Rev. 16:8-9

Darkness on Antichrist's kingdom

"...poured out his vial upon the seat of the beast; and his kingdom was full of darkness; and they gnawed their tongues for pain, and blasphemed the God of heaven because of their pains and their sores, and repented not of their deeds."
- Rev. 16:10-11

Euphrates dried up. World armies summoned to Armageddon for final battle

"...And the sixth angel poured out his vial upon the great river Euphrates; and the water thereof was dried up, that the way of the kings of the east might be prepared. And I saw three unclean spirits like frogs come out of the mouth of the dragon, and out of the mouth of the beast, and out of the mouth of the false prophet. For they are the spirits of devils, working miracles, which go forth unto the kings of the earth and of the whole world, to gather them to the battle of that great day of God Almighty." - Rev. 16:12-14

Quick Reminder Inserted

"...Behold, I come as a thief. Blessed is he that watcheth, and keepeth his garments, lest he walk naked, and they see his shame." - Rev. 16:15.

This reminder is to the seven churches (pre-tribulation) that Christ's coming and gathering of them will not be like the end of the tribulation, when the entire world gathers together in anticipation of battling the Lamb. The metaphor He uses is when a Temple guard was caught sleeping on the job, his boss would light his clothes on fire. This was the same metaphor and warning that Christ gave to His disciples - that His gathering of His church will be before the Tribulation, when people aren't expecting it. Once the Tribulation starts, Satan (and anyone who reads Revelation) will know how many days till Christ comes back. Christ's return at the end of the Tribulation will not be a surprise at all.

Armageddon (Rev. 14:20, 16:16)

World armies start assembling in Megiddo (Northern Israel), and work their way down to Jerusalem. It is not one battle site, it is a campaign. The actual battle is later, and detailed in chapter 19.

Global Earthquake & Hail

"...and there was a great earthquake, such as was not since men were upon the earth, so mighty an earthquake, and so great. And the great city was divided into three parts, and the **cities of the nations fell** ...And **every island fled away, and the mountains were not found.** And there fell upon men a great hail out of heaven, every stone about the weight of a talent: and men blasphemed God because of the plague of the hail; for the plague thereof was exceeding great." - Rev. 16:18-21

The hailstones are *"a talent weight."* A Hebrew talent was 114 lbs.

"...It is done." Rev. 16:17

There is probably no infrastructure still standing or untouched - dams have burst, highways buckled, bridges wrecked, rails tangled, runways cracked and pockmarked, lines downed, pipes broken, shorelines erased, debris and carnage everywhere. The pre-invasion bombardment has destroyed thousands of years of Satan's rule.

The Harlot Destroyed

The religious/political entity known as the whore (harlot) is destroyed by the ten kings. She is known as the whore for going after any false god. For a while they used her as a pantheon of false gods, and to help consolidate the world's religions. Now, as they move the world toward worshipping the antichrist, they must destroy their competition. While described in detail in this interlude, this event appears to take place around the midpoint of the Tribulation.

"...upon her forehead was a name written, MYSTERY, BABYLON THE GREAT, THE MOTHER OF HARLOTS AND ABOMINATIONS OF THE EARTH. And I saw the woman drunken with the blood of the saints, and with the blood of the martyrs of Jesus..." - Rev. 17:5-6

This entity is the embodiment, preserver, and promoter of all false gods from the time of early Babylon. She is also the greatest persecutor of the believers in Jesus Christ (the true church).

"...the ten horns which thou sawest are ten kings, which have received no kingdom as yet; but receive power as kings one hour with the beast. These have one mind, and shall give their power and strength unto the beast. These shall make war with the Lamb, and the Lamb shall overcome them ...the ten horns which thou sawest upon the beast, these shall hate the whore, and shall make her desolate and naked, and shall eat her flesh, and burn her with fire." - Rev. 17:12-16

Events Transpiring on Earth, John's perspective in Heaven.

▲ Babylon Destroyed

While the harlot was destroyed by the ten kings, historic Babylon will be destroyed by God, Himself. Sometime during the Tribulation, the Antichrist will start a rebuilding effort at historic Babylon - where the mystery of iniquity rebellion against God got started.

"*...I saw another angel come down from heaven, having great power; and the earth was lightened with his glory. And he cried mightily with a strong voice, saying,* **Babylon the great is fallen, is fallen***...*" - Rev. 18:1-2

"Come out of her, my people, that ye be not partakers of her sins, and that ye receive not of her plagues. For her sins have reached unto heaven, and God hath remembered her iniquities." - Rev. 18:4-5

'And Babylon, the glory of kingdoms, the beauty of the Chaldees' excellency, shall be as when God overthrew Sodom and Gomorrah." - Isaiah 13:19

"...her plagues come in one day, death, and mourning, and famine; and she shall be utterly burned with fire: for strong is the Lord God who judgeth her. ...for in one hour is thy judgment come." - Rev. 18:8,10

🌐 **Events Transpiring on Earth,** John's perspective in Heaven.

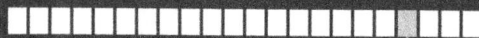

🐎 Christs Return

☁ In Heaven

Rev 19 - The multitude of His servants already in Heaven praise the Lord God (vs. 19:6) before He leaves Heaven to return to earth with them (19:11). His children *"which were in heaven"* ride with Him.

> *" ... I heard a great voice of much people in heaven, saying,* **Alleluia; Salvation, and glory, and honour, and power, unto the Lord our God: for true and righteous are his judgments..."** - Rev. 19:1-2

> *"...And I heard as it were the voice of a great multitude, and as the voice of many waters, and as the voice of mighty thunderings, saying,* **Alleluia: for the Lord God omnipotent reigneth."** - Rev. 19:6

> *"...Let us be glad and rejoice, and give honour to him: for the marriage of the Lamb is come, and his wife hath made herself ready.*
>
> *And to her was granted that she should be arrayed in fine linen, clean and white: for the fine linen is the righteousness of saints.*
>
> *And he saith unto me, Write, Blessed are they which are called unto the marriage supper of the Lamb."* - Rev. 19:7-9

The Beast **vs. The Lamb**

"...the spirits of devils, working miracles, which go forth unto the kings of the earth and of the whole world, to gather them to the battle of that great day of God Almighty." - Rev. 16:14

"These shall make war with the Lamb, and the Lamb shall overcome them: for he is Lord of lords, and King of kings: and they that are with him are called, and chosen, and faithful." - Rev. 17:14

"And I saw the beast, and the kings of the earth, and their armies, gathered together to make war against him that sat on the horse, and against his army." - Rev. 19:19

"And I saw heaven opened, and behold a white horse; and he that sat upon him was called **Faithful and True,** and in righteousness he doth judge and make war." - Rev. 19:11

"And the armies which were in heaven followed him upon white horses, clothed in fine linen, white and clean." - Rev. 19:14

"And out of his mouth goeth a sharp sword, that with it he should smite the nations: and he shall rule them with a rod of iron: and he treadeth the winepress of the fierceness and wrath of Almighty God." - Rev. 19:15

"And he hath on his vesture and on his thigh a name written,

KING OF KINGS, AND LORD OF LORDS
- Rev. 19:16

"...I saw an angel standing in the sun; and he cried with a loud voice, saying to all the fowls that fly in the midst of heaven, Come and gather yourselves together unto the supper of the great God; that ye may eat the flesh of kings, and the flesh of captains, and the flesh of mighty men, and the flesh of horses..."
- Rev. 19:17-18

Horses? (Rev. 19:17-18)

The Bible specifies that horses will be noticeably present at the Battle of Armageddon. In our day of tanks, fighter jets, jeeps, etc. it seems a bit archaic. Yet, when we consider that the entire globe just recently went through an earthquake that leveled cities and mountains (and also a global earthquake a few years ago), there is probably no infrastructure still standing that is normally needed to operate such technology (dams have burst, highways buckled, bridges wrecked, rails tangled, runways cracked, etc.). Aircraft carriers would probably be some of the primary victims from the 2nd Trumpet judgment.

Also, in conjunction with the years of infrastructure damage, by now fuel would be very precious and hard to transport. Horses (including donkeys, mules, etc.), on the other hand, would make perfect sense for transport under the conditions expected; they can traverse a variety of rough terrain, and carry equipment and supplies as well.

Because of these same logistical issues, and depravations by the previous years of war and natural disasters, heavy, mechanized weaponary probably won't be involved as well. Arms will probably be limited, spare parts limited, fuel scares, etc. The dynamics occuring in the world leading up to this battle will drastically change how this battle is equipped and deployed.

"And the beast was taken, and with him the false prophet that wrought miracles before him, with which he deceived them that had received the mark of the beast, and them that worshipped his image. These both were cast alive into a lake of fire burning with brimstone. And the remnant were slain with the sword of him that sat upon the horse, which sword proceeded out of his mouth: and all the fowls were filled with their flesh."
- Rev. 19:20-21

Armies destroyed with just the word out of Christ's mouth (Rev. 19:21). The battlefield, filled with blood, is 1,600 furlongs (about 200 miles) in size. Earth's rebellion is crushed like grapes in a winepress (19:15).

"And I saw an angel come down from heaven, having the key of the bottomless pit and a great chain in his hand. And he laid hold on the dragon, that old serpent, which is the Devil, and Satan, and bound him a thousand years, And cast him into the bottomless pit, and shut him up, and set a seal upon him, that he should deceive the nations no more..." - Rev. 20:1-3

1,000 yrs

"...till the thousand years should be fulfilled: and after that he must be loosed a little season." - Rev. 20:3

1,000 yr Millennial Kingdom (Zech. 14:16)

When Christ returns, most of Earth will be in a disaster zone state, especially after two global earthquakes. It will take years to rebuild infrastructure, cities, services, as well as clean up these areas.

"And from the time that the daily sacrifice shall be taken away, and the abomination that maketh desolate set up, there shall be a thousand two hundred and ninety days. Blessed is he that waiteth, and cometh to the thousand three hundred and five and thirty days." (Daniel 12:11). IF Sept. 23, 2017 is the day the desolation is set up, then 1290 days later would be Apr. 5th, 2021. 1335 days from Sept. 23, 2017 would be May 20th, 2021.

Kingdom Transition Time
It appears that these days mentioned past the return time refer to the time it takes for Christ's new rulers and governors to spread out across the globe, announce the victory, establish authority, and get the respective provinces set up. (Isaiah 2:2-4; 66:19; Zech 8:21-23).

While cities are being cleared and rebuilt, many will still live in simple conditions, using the implements of war from Armageddon as firewood. Scripture states they will be burning off this debris alone for seven years (Ezek. 39:9-10).

Scripture also details that some will be in full-time employment going around burying human remains - for seven months (Ezek. 39:12-16).

While it will take time to rebuild, it will also allow a clean, fresh start for mankind.

Satan's rule of the world is ended, and now Jesus Christ physically rules over mankind. The advancements during this time will make previous history pale - this is because Satan binds and suppresses, while Christ sets free.

The saints in Heaven return with Christ and stay to reign on the earth. *"the LORD my God shall come, and all the saints with thee."* - Zech 14:5

Jesus Christ Will Reign on Earth

- Jerusalem will be the world capital (Jer. 31).
- King David will serve as prince over Israel (Isa. 55:3-4; Jer. 30:9; Ezek. 34:23-24).
- The saints of the ages will also rule and reign, according to their rewards. Those who refused the mark of the beast will rule and reign with Christ (Daniel 11:32-35) in the various other nations and provinces as princes, and other levels of authority.

Those remaining from the Tribulation, (saved and unsaved, Zech. 14:16) will enter Christ's 1,000 kingdom on earth.

The First Resurrection
Those resurrected to life in this period. This includes those believers before Christ's earthly ministry, the saints dead from the start of the church through the Rapture, and the Tribulation saints that were martyred. Rev. 20:5

"And he shall judge among the nations, and shall rebuke many people: and they shall beat their swords into plowshares, and their spears into pruninghooks: nation shall not lift up sword against nation, neither shall they learn war any more." - Isaiah 2:4

Jerusalem will be the center of worship, and regular and constant pilgrimages will be made by those from all over the world (Isaiah 66:23).

The heathen will observe the Feast of Tabernacles every year, and it will be required (Zech 14:16).

Jerusalem will be greatly enlarged (Jer. 31:38-39).

"The wolf also shall dwell with the lamb, and the leopard shall lie down with the kid; and the calf and the young lion and the fatling together; and a little child shall lead them." - Isaiah 11:6

The Earth will once again be very fertile, yielding bountifully (Isaiah 30:23).

The Curse has been conquered, and will be lifted, returning Earth to Edenic state.

There will be a great outpouring of the Holy Spirit, with joy, gladness, and peace (Isa. 35:10; 51:11; Ezek. 11:19).

Lifespans will be greatly increased (Isa. 49:19-20; 65:20; Jer. 30:18-20). Death is still possible (Isa. 65:20).

Even though the world is like the Garden of Eden, sin is still in the heart. Christ will rule *"all nations with a rod of iron."* - Rev. 12:5. Many generations grow - many of whom only obey Christ unwillingly. Even though there is no doubt that there are no false gods, they still chose to rebel inwardly.

This inward rebellion by many eventually is made manifest at the end of the 1,000 years.

- -

"And when the thousand years are expired, Satan shall be loosed out of his prison, and shall go out to deceive the nations which are in the four quarters of the earth, Gog and Magog, to gather them together to battle: the number of whom is as the sand of the sea." - Rev. 20:7-8

Satan's armies, gathered from around the world, surround Jerusalem.

Fire from God out of heaven devours them (Rev. 20:9).

Satan cast into the Lake of Fire for evermore (Rev. 20:10).

- -

Why Does God Allow This Final Revolt?
While Scripture does not say, perhaps it is to openly prove that all the external blessings of God, open miracles and reign of God, and even mankind living in the perfect environment cannot change man's heart. Only accepting Christ's finished work on our behalf can redeem our heart on the inside and save us.

Judgment Day

"...I saw a great white throne, and him that sat on it, from whose face the earth and the heaven fled away; and there was found no place for them." - Rev. 21:1

HOLY ᐧ HOLY ᐧ HOLY

*"And I saw the dead, small and great, stand before God; and the books were opened: and another book was opened, which is the book of life: and the dead were judged out of those things which were written in the books, according to their works. ...**And whosoever was not found written in the book of life was cast into the lake of fire.**"* - Rev. 20:12,15

*"For by **grace** are ye saved through **faith**; and that not of yourselves: it is the **gift** of God: Not of works, lest any man should boast."* - Ephesians 2:8-9

The Second Resurrection

Only the unbelievers, ever since mankind's creation, are raised for this Last Judgment (Rev. 20:6). In a sense, their verdict has already been decided - that is why they are here; yet, the evidence must be presented, and final sentencing handed down. Not only did they choose not to have their name in the Book of Life, but the records of their works also show they are sinners. In this life, Jesus Christ offered to take their punishment, and successfully appeal their case (since He paid the way (John 3:16)), but they declined His offer, His payment, His grace, and His mercy.

> *"For there is one God, and **one mediator between God and men, the man Christ Jesus...**"* - I Timothy 2:5

The Antichrist, and his false prophet, will be the first ones sent to the Lake of Fire (19:20).

Satan will be tossed into the Lake of Fire at the end of the Millenial Kingdom (20:10).

Lake of Fire

The Lake of Fire was created for Satan and his fallen angels (Matthew 25:41) - because they rejected God and rebelled against Him; they did not want God telling them what to do, or to be in their life. Likewise, humans who also reject and choose to rebel against God and Christ will be allowed to join Satan, and have their life without God. That final choice is made in this life.

Wages
of sin
Rom. 6:23
Isaiah 64:6

How can I be sure my name is in the Book of Life?

"...all have sinned, and come short of the glory of God." Romans 3:23

*"...the wages of sin is **death**."*
Romans 6:23

*"But God commendeth his **love** toward us, in that while we were yet sinners, Christ died for us."*
Romans 5:8

*"...whosoever believeth in him should not perish, but have **eternal life**. For God so **loved** the world, that he gave his only begotten Son, that whosoever believeth in him should not perish, but have **everlasting life**."*
John 3:15-16

*"... if thou shalt confess with thy mouth the Lord Jesus, and shalt believe in thine heart that God hath raised him from the dead, **thou shalt be saved**."*
Romans 10:9

New Heaven & New Earth

"And he that sat upon the throne said, Behold, I make all things new." - Rev. 21:5

"And I saw a new heaven and a new earth: for the first heaven and the first earth were passed away..." - Rev. 21:1

At a distance, the city may appear like a giant prism and lustrous diamond.

The Lamb, the Light of the World, the symbolic golden lampstand, is now the light of the city and world by His glory **(Rev. 21:23).**

"And I saw no temple therein: for the Lord God Almighty and the Lamb are the temple of it." - Rev. 20:7-8

New Jerusalem

- The Holy City (Rev. 21:2; 22:19);
  The Heavenly Jerusalem (Heb. 11:16, 12:22), Mount Zion (Hebrews 12:22);
  The Bride, the Lamb's Wife (Rev. 21:9).
- 1,323 miles foursquare (Rev. 21:16).
  Three gates on each side, each gate a pearl Inscribed with one of the 12 tribes of Israel (Rev. 21:17,21). Jesus Christ is likened to the Pearl of Great Price (Matt 13:45).
  12 Foundations garnished with different precious stones, engraven with the names of the apostles (Rev. 21:14).
  Walls of diamond, and the city and street of pure, transparent gold (Rev. 21:18).

No Physical Barriers

"...and there was no more sea." - Rev. 21:1
The writer, John, was exiled on an island, and no doubt longed for when there would be no more sea.

Paradise Regained

The tree of life, once guarded by the cherubim in the Garden of Eden, is now available in the midst of the city, bearing 12 different fruits (Rev. 22:2).

Family & Friends

"...now I know in part; but then shall I know even as also I am known." - Rev. 21:4

No More Tears

"And God shall wipe away all tears from their eyes; and there shall be no more death, neither sorrow, nor crying, neither shall there be any more pain: for the former things are passed away." - Rev. 21:4

- All memories of the old world will be forgotten.

"Surely goodness and mercy shall follow me all the days of my life: and I will dwell in the house of the LORD for ever." - Psalm 23:6

"Brethren, I count not myself to have apprehended: but this one thing I do, forgetting those things which are behind, and reaching forth unto those things which are before, I press toward the mark for the prize of the high calling of God in Christ Jesus."

- Philippians 3:13-14

Table of Contents

144,000......................................78

666...12

Ahnenerbe...............................28

Anak...7

Anakims.....................................7

Antichrist.........13, 21, 72, 89-94, 98, 101, 119

Anunnaki.............................9, 24, 31

Apis..11

Ark of the Covenant..................20, 98

armour of God............................3

Ashtoreth / Ashtaroth..........10, 12, 14, 19

Ashur..10

Astarte......................................10

Baal, Bel................................10, 12, 18

Babel..................................9, 10

Baby Boomers.......................37-38

Babylon/ian............9, 21, 31, 84, 115

Babylonian, captivity..........11, 15, 19

Bashan.......................................7

Black Virgins...........................19

Blood Moons...................47, **55**

bloodline................................7, 24

Boomerang Generation...............40

brain....................................30-31

brazen serpent..........................20

bull, sacred...............................11

Cabbalism............................14, 15

calf, golden...............................11

Catholic/ism....................18, 19, 56, 96

China....................................84-85

Chemosh...............................11, 14

Chiun....................................11, 13

Christ's Gathering.. 16,34-35,64,66-69,112,121

Church, the true.............17, 64, 79, 87

Church, the false.........................18

churches, the seven................61-63

David's Shield..........................12

Draco / dragon.....................24, 100

dry bones, valley of...................33

earthquakes..........42, 77, 87, 113, 118, 120

Egypt..............................51-54, 56

elders, the church.......................65

Emims.......................................7

Enoch......................................49

Enuma Elish................................9

EU.................................21, 47, 91

Facebook..................................29

fallen angels.........7, 9, 24, 31, 84, 89, 94

famine..................................38, 74

Gehenna...................................11

generation(s)....................7, 36-41, 59

Generation Me..........................40

Generation X.............................39

Generation Y.............................40

Generation Z.............................41

giants...7

Gilgamesh, Epic of......................9

Goliath.......................................7

Gomorrah...................................8

Google......................................29

Hitler..............................13, 28, 91

hexagram.............................12, 13

Hollywood.................................31

Horus.......................................19

Ishtar...................10, 11, 18, 31, 104

Isis.............................10, 18, 19, 31

Islam...............................52, 56, 96

Israel, future prophecy.........51-55, 106

Israel, re-formed...............33, 38,43

Jerusalem.............32, 107, 122, 127

Jesus...16, 20, 32, 116-117, 121, 123, 125, 127

Judas.......................................26

Judgment Day..........................124

Laban's idols...............................9

Lot......................................8, 49-50

Lucifer, *see Satan*

Marduk.....................................10

mark, of the beast...............102-103

Mary.............................19, 20, 56

Mary, Islam..........................20, 56

Masonic...............................12, 25

Mengele, Josef...........................25

Merodach 10
Methuselah 49
microchip 5, 103
Millennial Generation 40
Millennial Kingdom 120
mind control, *see programming*
Molech 11, 12, 13, 14, 24, 102
moon, celestial 99
moon, god 10, 11
MTV Generation 39
Muslim, *see Islam*
mystery of Christ 1
mystery of iniquity 1, 2, 27
Nazi 13, 28, 37, 102
Nephilim, *see fallen angels*
Nimrod.. 10
Ninnar.. 10
Nisroch...9, 31
Noah 7, 49-50, 89
Nusku..9, 31
obelisk 18
Odin 13
Osiris 10, 19
pantheon 18
Pergamon Altar 4
Pergamon Museum 13
persecution 42, 76, 97, 102, 104-105
Peter Pan Generation 40
pinecone 18
programming / mind control 24, 25, 30-31
pyramids... 10
Queen of Heaven 10, 11, 14, 18, 20, 21, 104
Rapture, *see Christ's Gathering*
Remphan, star of....................................11, 12
rewards 57-58, 61-63, 121, 129
Samarra Bowl 13
Satan............ 10, 22, 83, 97, 102, 104, 119, 123
Satan, synagogue of...................................... 16
Saturn 10, 11, 13
secret societies 11, 16, 23-26

Semiramis 10
Solomon 14, 24
Solomon, Seal of 12
Shinar 9
signs fulfilled 42-48
Sodom 8, 50
Star of David, *see Star of Molech, Remphan*
Star of Molech 12, 102
Star Wars...31
stars, signs in the 48, 99-100
Stephen, martyr...12
Sumer 9
sun, celestial 99, 110
sun, god 10, 13, 18, 19
sun wheel 18, 19
swastika 13
Syria 52, 56, 94
Talisman of Saturn 12
Tammuz 19
Temple 14
Tetrad, Lunar 55
Thor 13
tower of Babel... 9
Teutonic Order...13
Thule Society...13
UFOs.. 93-95
understanding times.......................................1
Ur.. 9
Utnapishtim.. 9
Vatican 18, 19
Vril Society 13
War of the Worlds...31
watching 32-35
witnesses, two 87-88
Whore, The...21, 114
World War II 37
World War III 73-75
ying, yang 12
Zamzummims...7
Ziggurat 9, 10

www.ingramcontent.com/pod-product-compliance
Lightning Source LLC
Chambersburg PA
CBHW070835100426
42813CB00003B/626